transformed giving

CAMPAIGN HANDBOOK

transformed giving

realizing your church's full stewardship potential

CAMPAIGN HANDBOOK

A Stewardship Resource for Churches of All Sizes

TRANSFORMED GIVING
REALIZING YOUR CHURCH'S FULL STEWARDSHIP POTENTIAL

Copyright © 2006 by Abingdon Press

All rights reserved.

This book is printed on acid-free, elemental-chlorine–free paper.

Cover and page design by Joey McNair.
Art by Steve Cohen/FoodPix/Jupiterimages.

Campaign Kit (includes Campaign Handbook and Campaign Media)
ISBN–13: 978-0-687-33475-9
ISBN–10: 0-687-33475-6

Campaign Handbook
ISBN–13: 978-0-687-33427-8
ISBN–10: 0-687-33427-6

Campaign Media
ISBN–13: 978-0-687-33437-7
ISBN–10: 0-687-33437-3

12   13   14   15   10   9   8   7   6   5   4   3   2

MANUFACTURED IN THE UNITED STATES OF AMERICA

contents

Contents

foreword

Dear friend,

Welcome to *Transformed Giving* and its comprehensive, churchwide study, *Treasures of the Transformed Life*. This powerful study is one that can have long-lasting impact for both you and your entire church family.

I've been a pastor long enough to know that none of us really has all the answers. But we do have the opportunity to learn from each other on the road we're all walking; and it's my hope that something I've discovered along the way might be of use to you and your church.

This campaign handbook is the result of trial and error within my own congregation, Frazer Memorial United Methodist Church in Montgomery, Alabama, as well as general tried-and-true stewardship strategies. At Frazer, we have incorporated annual forty-day stewardship campaigns for several years now, and the results have been phenomenal. Generous giving has become part of the overall atmosphere of our body, and we are truly blessed with a congregation in which every member acts as a minister.

As you integrate the ideas from *Transformed Giving* and *Treasures of the Transformed Life* into your own church, may you find that you move forward as a unified, mighty team—one with God at the head; may you find new levels of commitment among your entire congregation; and may you know that there's always more to learn and experience. We've certainly seen these things at Frazer, and it's been a joy to watch God work.

Our prayers are with you as you move ahead on your journey into *Transformed Giving*!

Sincerely,
John Ed Mathison

chapter 1

what *transformed* *giving* is all about

I t's time to get excited.

The journey you've begun is so much more than just a forty-day milemarker. Instead, it's a path that can lead your entire congregation to greater fulfillment, joy, purpose, and destiny. And this handbook—combined with prayer—will provide everything you need to know along the way.

And speaking of prayer, let's take a moment to stop and pray right now. There's not much point in trying to do God's work without getting God involved right from the start. The pastor or stewardship committee chair should lead the committee in prayer:

> Compassionate Lord,
>   We thank you for the great opportunities for growth that lie before us. We praise you that you are taking us on a journey with you—one that can reap an incredible harvest for our families, our congregation, and our community. Help us

to press into you, to see more of you, and to learn everything that you want to teach us in the coming days.

We give you thanks in the mighty name of your son, Jesus, our savior. Amen.

money, money, money

If one of your key motivations for investing in this study is money, that's quite all right. Churches need it for community outreach, benevolence programs, staff salaries, and even just keeping the lights on in the building. But if you're like many churches, there's a marked difference in the congregation between supporting the efforts of the church and actually supporting it with cash. There are just so many other things on which people can spend their money, and unfortunately, there's a lack of understanding about the importance of tithes and offerings.

In our individualistic culture, people don't like to be told what to do—and they certainly don't like to be told what to do with their money. They worked hard for it, and it represents an element of control.

This is nothing new. Even in biblical times, when the marketplace was nothing like it is today, people still had to be reminded that "wherever your treasure is, there your heart and thoughts will also be" (Matt. 6:21). It is such an important concept—back then, just as it is now—that Jesus actually spoke about money more than any other topic in the Bible.

So why aren't today's churches doing the same?

All too often, the church is seen as having its hand out, asking for more than people want to give. And yes, sacrifice is a basic tenet of Christianity, but wouldn't it be nice if members of the congregation gave willingly and enthusiastically, rather than defensively and begrudgingly? It can happen, but there's something that must be understood first: If you want people to give their money—and to experience the rich benefits of God's provision and increased faith—then you've also got to teach them to give of themselves.

Find a person who willingly gives financial gifts to the church, and you'll also see someone who understands the importance of prayer. Find someone with a rich prayer life, and you'll see someone who feels compelled to regularly attend worship services. Find someone who attends every Sunday, and you'll see that the person is also motivated to serve. It all fits together beautifully—just the way God intended.

So maybe you don't see many people in your congregation at that level of commitment. But they can be, and this resource will show you exactly how it can happen.

the perfect lead-in to commitment sunday

Transformed Giving is designed to be a comprehensive study that will inspire church members in many different ways, on many different levels. The idea is that the messages are simple and yet profound, and are repeated enough that church members won't be able to miss them. Daily readings, for example, will be reinforced in weekly small group sessions or class studies, as well as through the pastor's sermons and a series of other communications for a period of six weeks.

The study is designed to be incorporated into the church's annual stewardship campaign, with the last message given on Commitment Sunday. By that time, members of the congregation will have studied the importance of individually giving of their time, prayers, acts of service, and finances, and Commitment Sunday offers a moment for the congregation to bring it all together under one corporate umbrella of commitment. The actual commitment also gives church members an opportunity to apply what they've learned long after the study is completed, committing their support in these key four areas for the weeks, months, and years to come.

Combining a stewardship campaign with a churchwide study may seem to be a novel idea. You may not be familiar with some of the aspects of such a program—perhaps you have no experience with a stewardship campaign, churchwide study, or small group Bible study. That's not a problem. This program shows you how to incorporate all those things with a very essential element—unity.

Remember that there's strength in numbers. Involving your entire congregation in moving toward a focused goal can be a powerful thing indeed. It will build bridges where there currently are none, and offer opportunities for discussion, prayer, and encouragement among people who might not previously have found anything in common. Members of your congregation will find open doors for talking about things like faith, money, and service. Most important, the unified church is one in which the enemy can't win. With everyone's eyes focused on the goal, there will less emphasis on complaining, gossip, negativity, and other potentially damaging attitudes among members.

letting go and letting God

At the very core of the *Treasures of the Transformed Life* study is a shift in overall thinking, a transition from fear to confidence.

It's all too easy to put our confidence in a paycheck, or to see our employer as our provider. But that's not God's best. Scripture actually has a lot to say on the topic. Matthew 6:32–33, for example, promises us:

> Your heavenly Father already knows all your needs, and he will give you all you need from day to day if you live for him and make the Kingdom of God your primary concern.

There's also Psalm 23, which begins: "The Lord is my shepherd; I have everything I need," and 1 Timothy 6:17, which urges:

Tell those who are rich in this world not to be proud and not to trust in their money, which will soon be gone. But their trust should be in the living God, who richly gives us all we need for our enjoyment.

For a variety of reasons, too many of us are afraid to commit our time or our finances, even when we believe in that to which we're being asked to commit. We are all busy people. Our time is precious. We may fear we don't have enough time to give some of it away in the service of others. We may hoard it as we would money, fearful about having enough for our own needs.

In the parable of the good Samaritan, Jesus tells us to look at his example and do likewise. This takes time. Galatians 5:22 reminds us of the fruit of the Spirit—particularly love, kindness, goodness, and gentleness—that we are to be developing. Philippians 2:4 exhorts us: "Don't think only about your own affairs, but be interested in others, too, and what they are doing."

The most practical way to develop in these areas is in relationship with and in the service of others. The irony is that, as we focus on others' needs, we get our needs met. Author and speaker Zig Ziglar says, "You can get everything in life you want if you help enough other people get what they want." Proverbs 11 tells us that the merciful, kind man benefits himself, and he who waters will himself be watered (v. 11: 17, 25 AMP). Jesus, of course, said it is better to give than to receive.

Getting this message through to a congregation, however, can be a tough sell. Without a willingness to let go and let God, or to release what we hold so tightly (whether it is our time, attendance, prayers, or money), we're not given a full opportunity to see God work. If we can meet all of our needs on our own, what do we need God for? Teaching our church family to tithe, give offerings, pray, and serve allows them the chance to experience God's provision in new and miraculous ways and to deepen their understanding of faith and trust.

Of course, this also offers great results for the church as a corporate body. Not only is the level of faith increased but also the amount of funds available for church programs and ministries and the number of people available to serve will increase. A church in which each person gives and serves according to the Lord's leading is a church in which anything is possible.

what's included

Let's get started with a brief overview of the *Transformed Giving* program kit's components. We'll go into more detail later, but this will at least help you understand the variety of resources at your fingertips and will give you a reference point as you continue reading this handbook.

- *Treasures of the Transformed Life—Satisfying Your Soul's Thirst for More:* This book is the backbone of the study. Broken into forty chapters for daily study by individuals, it dives into the depths of prayer, presence, gifts, and service.
- *Participant's Workbook* or *Leader's Guide* to *Treasures of the Transformed Life:* The workbook includes six weekly lessons to help facilitate discussions in small groups or Sunday school classes. It also guides accountability for the individual readings. The *Leader's Guide* contains the same text as the workbook, but it includes a DVD to share with groups.
- Media Kit
  - CD-ROM Toolkit
    - Sample sermons: One sermon associated with each week is provided by Mathison. They can be used as a jumping-off point for your church's pastor to discuss the topics with your own congregation.

– Bulletin inserts: Articles for insertion into your church bulletins can help create excitement and unity among the congregation.
– Newsletter columns: These can be incorporated into mid-week newsletters to keep members of the congregation up-to-date, motivated, and on-target.
– Various other materials: Includes sample letters, program graphics, and forms that support the campaign.

- DVDs
  – Weekly DVDs included with the *Leader's Guide*: Six brief segments on the DVD feature John Ed Mathison introducing small groups and Sunday school classes to each topic at the opening of weekly meetings.
  – *Transformed Giving as a Group Effort—John Ed Mathison Talks to the Stewardship Committee:* A motivational message by Mathison directed toward the stewardship committee.
  – *Transformed Giving WILL Transform Your Church—Pastor-to-Pastor, John Ed Mathison Talks Frankly About Stewardship:* An explanatory message with Mathison talking to the church's pastor about the challenges and fruits of stewardship.
  – *Drawing Out Effective Testimonies:* A brief demonstration modeling how your church can use personal testimonies to encourage and inspire the entire congregation.

The study will take forty days for the congregation to complete. Of course, it will take a little more time than that to pull it off from an organizational standpoint. That's what this book is all about. You'll find suggested timelines, tips, and more in the following pages, but don't be afraid to make this campaign your own. Nobody knows your church like your church's leadership, so there may be places that need to be tweaked for a better fit. Go for it. With God on your side, you will certainly win.

the forty of the forty-day study

The Israelites wandered in the desert for forty years (Deut. 8:2–5); Jesus was tempted by Satan for forty days (Mark 1:13); Noah built his ark in preparation for a rain that lasted forty days and forty nights (Gen. 7:4); and Moses was on Mount Sinai for forty days and forty nights speaking with God about commandments and laws (Exod. 24:18).

Throughout the Bible, the number forty is used to denote a season or preparation of trial. Forty days is roughly six weeks, and even in today's culture, it's not that difficult to find books with titles like *Six Weeks to a Simpler Lifestyle*, *Forty Days to Personal Revolution*, and even *Six Weeks to a Hollywood Body*.

It's not that the number of days is magical. On a practical level, six weeks is the length of time experts say it takes to develop a new habit. A forty-day study, then, divided into six weeks, can be long enough to make a significant difference in the habits of your congregation.

The span of six weeks isn't so long that people will lose interest. It's brief enough to always see the proverbial light at the end of the tunnel, or the goal everyone's working toward. It's also a familiar marker of growth. Remember six-week progress reports from school? Think of this study, then, as a crash course in growing closer to God. At its close, the progress will be apparent to all.

Imagine what your church could be like if every member was committed to daily study, and each one was on the same page with everyone else—literally. What would it be like if members came to Sunday worship with expectancy and excitement, knowing what topic would be discussed?

Imagine, too, the possibilities of continuing that sense of anticipation long after the forty-day campaign was complete. Since this campaign finishes with the filling out of commitment cards and service commitment forms, it's aimed at serving as a new beginning rather than an end.

The best part is that everyone likes being part of a team and working toward common goals. As such, *Treasures of the Transformed Life* can help your church family grow in unity, creating long-lasting relationships along the way.

The idea of forty days, then, isn't arbitrary—even if this is the first time you've seen it linked to a stewardship campaign. It is simply a period of time to which people can commit, having a defined goal in sight. And once the good habits of increased prayer, godly introspection, willingness to serve, and understanding of tithes and offerings are set, they can continue for a lifetime and propel your church family into a truly world-changing congregation.

chapter 3

the overall
philosophy

A savvy businesswoman once said that if you want people to commit to an idea or organization, you've got to make them feel important. Everyone wants to feel that their involvement matters. Some organizations try to accomplish that goal with awards and rewards, with recognition and promotions. But in a church, the best way to make people feel important and appreciated is to help them learn how important they are to God, and how much his appreciation matters. When members of a congregation are secure in their standing with the one who made them, they're much less likely to seek approval elsewhere; striving and jockeying for position go right out the window.

It can happen with a study like *Treasures of the Transformed Life*. Since the study is based on the concept of giving one's whole self to God and not just one's finances, it can help individual members of the congregation find new levels of intention, appreciation, and ultimately joy in serving others and serving God. Letting people know that their time and efforts are every bit as important as their money raises their levels of confidence and self-worth.

dr. john ed mathison

Transformed Giving began with Dr. John Ed Mathison, pastor of Frazer Memorial United Methodist Church in Montgomery, Alabama. When Mathison became pastor there more than thirty years ago, he discovered that the church had been through a financial campaign that had failed to achieve the desired effects. Members of the congregation became disillusioned, and some even felt they had been taken advantage of. And yet, unfortunately, there was still money to be raised.

After much prayer, Mathison and some leaders developed a plan that could be incorporated into his church's annual stewardship campaign. Instead of just asking people to fill out financial commitment cards at the end of the campaign, he took the spotlight off of the money. He asked people to fill out commitment cards that listed areas of service in addition to the monetary commitments. He began preaching about the fact that every single member was important, and that every member should be involved in some area of ministry.

Mathison's church has since flourished. Its membership has gone from fewer than four hundred to more than eighty-six hundred. Its annual budget is now more than $10 million—and that budget is met each year. Joyfully. Expectantly. No longer do members feel that the church only wants them for their money. Instead, there's an understanding that each person's unique talents are essential to the success of the church. Of course, no church is perfect, but Frazer enjoys a much higher-than-average level of participation in all aspects of ministry—including financial. Obviously, something is working at Frazer—something worth study and reproduction.

the idea of commitment

It's important to note that *Transformed Giving* is no magic bullet. It's not an answer to every problem that might plague your congregation. It is, however, an opportunity for members to understand their worth in God's eyes in a whole new way.

The study itself is based on the principles of prayer, presence, gifts, and service. It begins, however, by helping people realize their innate areas of dissatisfaction. As discussed in *Treasures of the Transformed Life*, great pain comes when we're empty. It may be because we recognize a deep-seated longing for something, or more likely, we try all sorts of ways of satisfying our longing without realizing what we really need. Sometimes we've been wounded by life, so we've given up trying to be happy. Sadly, many people are just going through the motions of living.

There are individuals in your congregation who fall into each of those categories. This study, then, meets them wherever they are in their walk with God. Even if they believe everything's fine, it can help them realize there's always more they can receive.

From the beginning, the study dives into the idea that God is committed to us, and that he expects us to be committed to him as well as others in our church family. The first week talks about the importance of every person doing his or her part, and discuss how each person was uniquely designed to fulfill a special role in God's heart and plan.

Since the forty-day study is divided into daily readings, the last reading of each week serves as a review. Key concepts are repeated, ensuring that they stick before moving on to the next topic.

the focus on prayer

The second week of the study focuses on prayer. Prayer is presented simply as a conversation with God, not something

scary or intimidating. Throughout the study, the book incorporates a water theme; the living water that comes through regular
connection with God through prayer is seen as the very thing
that helps us grow and flourish.

The week's lessons describe prayer not just as a list of things
we want, but as a two-way conversation through which we gain
insight, guidance, peace, and joy. It covers the aspects of part-
nering with God in his work and the way prayer allows us to be
more like Jesus as we spend time with God. One of the lessons
includes a simple pattern for prayer using the fingers of the
hand as a guide. Prayer, then, can be an easy-to-develop habit
rather than a daunting mystery.

By the time the second week is over, church members
could have a new understanding of the importance of praying
for others, praying for the church, and praying for the people
outside it.

the importance of presence

Next, *Treasures of the Transformed Life* moves on to the
topic of presence. It teaches that every member of God's
team has an essential part to play, and that regularly showing
up on Sunday mornings is part of that role. We need to
understand, the book says, that church just isn't the same
when we're not there. We matter. Indeed, we miss something
when we're absent; but just as important, the church misses
out, too.

Subsequent chapters during the third week establish the
church as God's family, with God at the head as Father. Being
part of that family means not only are we called individually by
name, but we're expected to regularly show up at the family
table for mealtime.

There are, of course, benefits to being part of a loving
family, one in which people are loved, accepted, forgiven, and

encouraged to grow. It's the kind of family that people outside the church long for, and the kind of love that allows us to bring others under the umbrella of God's love. Just like a typical family, the church family also has an opportunity to multiply.

the need for gifts

It may seem odd that the financial aspect is not the final part of the study leading up to Commitment Sunday. But placed as they are in the middle of the *Transformed Giving* campaign, the chapters on tithes and offerings simply fit into the entire study as a portion of the greater focus—to help people commit their lives, not just their pocketbooks.

These chapters, however, get down to the brass tacks of the matter. Tithing is clearly defined as giving 10 percent of one's income, and an offering is anything beyond that. There's no beating around the bush here; as says the quote from Thornton Wilder: "Money is like manure; it's not worth a thing unless it's spread around encouraging young things to grow."

These are not, however, heavy-handed chapters full of shoulds. Rather, the tithe is presented as an opportunity to help God do his work, and a chance for us to grow in faith and dependence on God to meet all of our needs. Giving back to God is a privilege, rather than a duty, and keeping money from God is a sign of misguided priorities. God, in his amazing and mysterious provision, blesses us in a variety of ways when we learn to trust him with every aspect of our lives—including our financial resources.

the benefits of service

Week five hones in on service, which in the body of Christ is like water to the human body. It offers refreshment and sustenance, and provides lubrication for our joints to improve flexibility, fuel for our muscles to increase strength, and movement in our blood so the heart remains connected to the brain. All that, plus something more: Service in the body of Christ allows us to be more like Jesus, the greatest servant of all.

Anyone who's been in a congregation for any length of time, however, knows that a couple of problems often exist. First, there's that traditional 80/20 split, in which 80 percent of the work is done by 20 percent of the people, leading to frustration on the part of those who aren't in service and burnout on the part of those who are. And then there's the problem of people not knowing how or where to serve.

Treasures of the Transformed Life covers both fronts. First, by encouraging every member to be in some area of ministry, the burdens of church work are more easily shared. And second, by offering people help in figuring out where they might be best placed, it helps members of the church family get involved in ways that are meaningful and rewarding to them.

bringing it home

The final week of the study is the one that brings it all home before Commitment Sunday. Here's where members of the congregation will take stock of where they currently are, as well as where they'd like to be. Elements of previous weeks are woven into the daily readings, encouraging members of the church family to see Commitment Sunday as a beginning instead of an end. The week also covers the importance of sharing your faith with others, a realistic definition of perfection, and being as passionate about the future as we are about today. The study closes with direct questions about the reader's readiness to commit in areas of prayer, presence, gifts, and service.

the most important commitment of all

There's one other thing it's important to note before your church begins its campaign. Some church leadership may be hesitant to ask its members specifically where they stand in their commitment to Jesus, lest they offend.

On the contrary, the *Treasures of the Transformed Life* study doesn't take anything for granted. An appendix, referred to in the first week, includes an explanation and prayer for accepting Jesus as Lord and Savior. If the person reading it is doing so for the first time, they're instructed to let someone else know.

Don't be surprised if *Transformed Giving* results in changes and salvations among your church body because it's designed to meet people wherever they are, and some people may not be exactly where you think.

the role of leadership

For the bus to get anywhere, somebody has to drive it. And in the case of *Transformed Giving*, the one driving the bus won't necessarily be the pastor. Instead, the majority of the effort will come from the stewardship committee. Even if your church is small, it's important to consider developing such a committee; it can take the pressure off of the pastor, as well as help develop a level of peer acceptance when it comes to things like committing to attendance, service, giving, and prayer. In most cases, members of the congregation will be much more likely to respond favorably to needs presented by their peers than to any pressure from the pastor.

Now, this is not to say that the pastor's role is diminished when it comes to stewardship. The pastor should be in regular contact with the stewardship committee leader; should offer theological and biblical counsel as needed; and should talk about how God meets us as we give of ourselves, our time, our prayers, and our finances. The pastor can set a good example for the congregation by regularly giving of his or her own finances and openly talking about money, tithes, offerings, and stewardship.

Developing a stewardship committee also gives the pastor the option of not knowing how much money individual members of the congregation give. Pastors who choose to distance themselves from specific knowledge of individual giving levels have greater freedom in their pastoral ministry. Allowing trusted lay leadership or other church staff to work with the specific financial commitments gives the pastor the option of not knowing the information.

The stewardship committee doesn't have to be a large group, especially if the congregation isn't large. But it is important that it's made up of a cross-section of members to ensure that different economic groups are fairly represented. Don't make the mistake of putting only the wealthiest folks on the committee, and expect that they'll be able to understand the needs of the congregation as a whole. A single mother struggling to make ends meet, for example, brings a completely different voice to the table than a successful entrepreneur.

wanted: generosity

The choice of who should be involved begins with a search for those with generous hearts. Chances are, you already know who they are. They're not necessarily the ones with the most cash, but they are they ones with an infectious attitude of selflessness, always willing to put other people's needs before their own.

In addition, look for members who are enthusiastic about church and spiritual growth. They'll be the ones who get excited about learning new truths, digging into the depths of

God's Word, and sharing with others what God has done in their lives.

You might also consider people who have financial work experience. This is not to say they're chosen solely for that reason, but an understanding of investments and the way money works can be a great asset to any team.

In addition, look for members who aren't afraid to dream big. Any successful stewardship committee needs both people who can see the big picture and the ones who can figure out the details to make it happen. Too much of one side or the other won't get you anywhere. Visionaries can offer excitement and possibility, while the detail folks can balance it out with practicality and planning.

Finally, resist the temptation to only fill the committee with seasoned church members and traditional leaders. Too often, church leadership can become stale or tired when the same people attempt to implement the church's programs. The committee can also provide an entry into leadership for newer church members. It can be a chance for them to grow into future front-runners, rubbing shoulders with those who are already in positions of authority and learning along the way. They can also bring fresh ideas to the table and maintain a voice with their peers. Remember, your more seasoned members may welcome an opportunity to serve in some other capacity.

following the leader

The first person that should be chosen for any committee is its leader, and that's a decision to be considered with much prayer. The leader should offer insight, accountability, and vision for the entire church body—not just the committee—so it's important that you carefully consider all the talents and skills that your potential candidates offer. It might help to come up with a job description for the leader so it's easier to see who fits. A list of desirable traits, for example, could include:

- evidence of a consistent Christian walk, displayed through commitment to attendance, tithing, service, and prayer
- a heart turned toward God and to living a clean, holy, and just life
- leadership/managerial skills
- humility and a teachable spirit
- honesty and trustworthiness
- enthusiasm for growing the church and congregation
- confidence about the connection between a Christian's money and his devotion to God—and a willingness to promote it
- a positive relationship with the pastor
- a positive reputation within the congregation
- previous experience in working with church fund-raising, stewardship or development campaigns (not necessary, but helpful)

Obviously, the leader should also be willing to lead. Most stewardship committees meet about once a month throughout the year, probably more in the months leading up the church's annual stewardship campaign. As the chair of the stewardship committee, then, the chosen leader would be responsible for planning and facilitating the meetings; helping appoint committee members; delegating and following up on assigned tasks; regularly reporting progress to the pastor; coordinating with other church committees; helping develop and implement the church budget; promoting stewardship throughout the congregation; and offering a personal example of commitment.

How much time all this will take depends on a number of factors, including the leader's ability to delegate, the committee's willingness to participate, the size and intricacy of the church budget, and the amount of confidence the pastor places in the committee chair. At any rate, it is not a position to be taken lightly.

the role of the committee

The stewardship committee does a lot more than just spearhead the *Transformed Giving* campaign. Anyone knows that programs and facilities require money, so the committee actually serves as a dream team for helping guide the path of the overall church. The committee must be clear on the vision of the pastor and be enthusiastic about helping carry it out.

In regard to this particular study, the committee also has an opportunity to help people grow in their perceptions of commitment through time, service, and prayer. It's an opportunity to affect not only the outcome of the church's annual budget but also scriptural foundations for generations to come. To prevent members of the committee from being overloaded, delegation is essential. Various roles might include:

- *Book distribution coordinator.* Develop a sales/distribution plan, help determine whether the books and workbooks are underwritten by the church or have the cost passed onto recipients, and develop a master checklist of all church families.

  If your church chooses to give thank-you gifts to members who turn in commitment cards and service commitment forms, the book distribution coordinator could have responsibility for distributing the gifts as well.

- *Small group coordinator.* Work with the education department leadership for Sunday school/small group studies, recruit small group leaders for short-term studies, heavily promote the study for full congregational participation, determine the quantity of resources to order, train small group leaders, coordinate the program with youth leadership, and ensure the availability of DVD players for Sunday school/small group meetings.

- *Volunteer commitment coordinator.* Work with individual church committees to develop the service commitment materials, develop a method for recording volunteer's responses, and communicate volunteer responses to appropriate church leaders for follow-up and eventual integration into the specified ministry areas.

- *Communications coordinator.* Work with church staff to coordinate mailings, newsletter text, and bulletin inserts; hang posters and distribute materials for the program; and communicate with church Webmaster (if applicable) regarding possible online elements.

- *Print resources coordinator.* Develop a schedule for all printed components, review the CD-ROM toolkit for program-furnished graphics, customize or develop new graphics as appropriate, draft/edit/design/adapt all printed components, and establish print quantities and secure printing.

- *Prayer coordinator.* Recruit participants for continual prayer throughout the forty-day period and coordinate a prayer vigil to commence twenty-four hours prior to Commitment Sunday.

- *Testimony coordinator.* Recruit church members to give personal testimony related to the study during each week of the campaign.

- *Follow-up coordinator.* Obtain lists of individuals who have not returned commitment cards or service commitment forms and ensure that follow-up letters are sent to those individuals.

- *Comparative study coordinator.* Gather statistics for comparison before and after the campaign.

- *Hospitality coordinator.* Make arrangements for a leadership prayer dinner (if your church opts to do one) and coordinate refreshments/decorations for Commitment Sunday.

how the
campaign works

At the heart of the *Transformed Giving* campaign, obviously, is the individual reading of *Treasures of the Transformed Life*. It's only through reading the book that members of the congregation can personally apply the principles to their lives. As such, every effort should be made to put books in the hands of members, and to encourage participation across all levels.

Different churches might go about this in different ways. Regardless, the best bet is to create an atmosphere in which people will truly feel left out if they're not participating. Church leadership should be encouraged to talk up the campaign in the days leading to its start, during the six weeks it takes place, and especially on Commitment Sunday. Rather than presenting the campaign as a requirement, however, introduce it as an exciting, potentially life-changing event not to be missed. You'll find a number of resources on the CD-ROM toolkit that will help you do that, including fun bulletin inserts and letters the pastor or the stewardship committee chair can sign and send directly to members of the congregation. But don't be afraid to be creative. Incorporate your church sign, consider hanging posters or banners, and if your church has something like a drama ministry, ask it to prepare a skit or two to be presented to the congregation.

Remember: The higher the expectancy of the congregation, the more likely they are to see God move in and among them.

keeping the goal in sight

Throughout the campaign, don't forget to emphasize that it will end with a commitment. As the campaign progresses, continue the countdown to Commitment Sunday, but be careful that it's not seen as simply a day for financial commitments. Rather, it's a time for commitment in service, prayer, attendance, and finances. Money is only part of the picture. Continue to emphasize the fact that God—and the church—wants every aspect of each member's life, not just his or her cash.

As far as the financial and service commitments are concerned, the congregation will have an opportunity to learn the joys of generosity. Be open about the importance of tithes and offerings, and of service and presence. If you, as a leader, have any reservations about asking people to fully participate, work through those reservations now.

group discussions

In addition to the individual study of *Treasures of the Transformed Life*, group discussion during Sunday school or small group meetings is a key aspect of the *Transformed Giving* campaign. This element builds bridges between members, and it helps establish common ground.

First, the *Participant's Workbook* offers a review of key concepts so they're not forgotten over the course of the week. Repetition can greatly aid in learning, so this step helps ensure that those key concepts are established before the next topic is introduced.

Group discussion also allows church members to hear other viewpoints. Those who are lacking faith in certain areas, for example, might find encouragement through others who are a little further along. The group meetings, which are clearly outlined in both the *Participant's Workbook* and the *Leader's Guide*, also incorporate opportunities for the participants to break into even smaller groups and share on a more personal level. This builds intimacy as well as humility as members learn to be more open with their thoughts.

Again, the *Participant's Workbook* and the *Leader's Guide* clearly outline the format for each meeting, and also give tips for first-time leaders on facilitating discussion. The meetings will run most smoothly, however, when the leaders are familiar with the key concepts and book chapters and are willing to rely on God for guidance. Pre-meeting prayer can definitely change the course of the gathering, and leaders should be chosen based on their ability to follow the lead of the Holy Spirit as much as their ability to help people learn.

The meetings are designed to last from forty-five minutes to an hour, so they can easily be covered in a traditional Sunday school format. Should your church have small group meetings at other times during the week, however, that's another option for group study. Suggestions for incorporating that into the campaign timeline are included.

If there's any question about the efficacy of small groups, keep in mind that Jesus did most of his work in small groups. Small groups and Sunday school classes offer intimacy, a chance for everyone to share and grow, and a safe place for people to participate. If your church doesn't currently offer small groups or Sunday school classes, the *Treasures of the Transformed Life* study is an excellent opportunity to start or expand participation in such programs. Many individuals may choose to continue their group meetings with new topics and studies.

the pastor's role

Each Sunday during the campaign, the pastor will present a message that incorporates the key concepts of the previous week's readings. The CD-ROM toolkit includes sample sermons written by John Ed Mathison, which can easily be used as a jumping-off point for the pastor in preparing his or her own messages.

The best-case scenario, however, is for the church pastor to read through each week's lessons and craft a personal message based on the insight learned. This is recommended for a number of reasons: First, it will give the messages a personal touch, and will allow members of the congregation to see that the entire church family really is in the campaign together, including the pastor. It will also demonstrate that no matter how mature we become in our walk with the Lord, we always have more to learn. This gives the pastor an opportunity to model unity and new ways of looking at tried-and-true ideas.

Beyond that, however, a pastor who crafts original messages has the opportunity to gear them toward the specific needs and challenges of the congregation. One church might find attendance issues its biggest concern; another might be challenged by a lack of consistent financial support; and yet another might have trouble encouraging people to step into acts of service. Regardless, the campaign covers them all and allows the pastor to mold messages that can speak to the heart.

But the pastor's role doesn't end there.

The CD-ROM toolkit also includes sample letters that can be sent from the pastor and/or stewardship committee chair to the congregation. One encourages participation before the study begins, and another is designed to be mailed to church members along with commitment cards and service commitment forms a few weeks before Commitment Sunday. But that's only the beginning. It's crucial for members of the congregation to see the pastor actually involved in the process and excited about it on a personal level. Otherwise, the campaign comes across as something that the stewardship committee has concocted simply to raise funds.

The pastor is the one who has the opportunity to lead the flock by personal example, which is always easier for people to follow. Keep the focus on "us" and "we" rather than on "you."

john ed mathison's lead

Throughout the study, there's a name and face that will become familiar to members of your church family: John Ed Mathison's. In addition to writing the text, Mathison has prepared DVD messages for this kit. They allow church leaders and lay members of the congregation to experience Mathison speaking straight from his heart. The DVD created for the pastor features Mathison in conversation with a fellow pastor. They discuss the concept of stewardship, the importance of leading by example, and the method of forming a stewardship committee. Mathison also shares background about his own church and its encouraging experiences with forty-day studies. Remember, John Ed Mathison hasn't always pastored a large church—his congregation had four hundred members when he began applying the principles incorporated into this *Transformed Giving* campaign.

A DVD presentation for the stewardship committee positions the committee as a dream team that can offer the church family both inspiration and the mechanics for getting things done. The DVD also includes testimony from someone whose life has been enriched by participation in such a committee.

Granted, members of the general congregation won't see the DVDs developed for the pastor and stewardship committee. They will, however, watch brief introductory DVD messages featuring Mathison at the start of each Sunday school/small group meeting. These help set the tone for discussions, provide consistency, and allow participants to hear Mathison's personal insights on the key concept for each week in the study.

testimony time

The media kit includes one more DVD segment, but this one warrants further explanation. Mathison created this DVD message to show others the importance of incorporating personal testimonies throughout the campaign—and beyond Commitment Sunday.

He has found that using an interview technique to elicit testimonies delivers stronger, more memorable testimonies. It also makes giving a testimony easier on the individual speaking. Mathison prefers this approach because it is less stressful for those giving the testimony and also helps ensure that the message they are trying to communicate is heard. Mathison models how to use that interview technique to guide people into succinct stories of what God has done in their lives.

At Mathison's church, testimonies are sometimes given in person on Sunday mornings, and sometimes they're played for the congregation on prerecorded DVDs. Using prerecorded testimonies is really helpful with multiple services and also allows for illustration of whatever the person is discussing. A testimony about serving, for example, might be accompanied by video footage showing the speaker working in the children's ministry.

For the purpose of the *Transformed Giving* campaign, however, feel free to keep things simple. Place a member of the stewardship committee in charge of finding and scheduling those who are willing to speak. Work in consultation with the pastor who will lead the interview. Incorporate one testimony during the worship service each week of the study, focusing on testimonies that directly relate to the churchwide study of the *Treasures of the Transformed Life* book. Sharing testimonies helps generate excitement for the campaign and encourages people who are not yet fully committed to dive in.

commitment cards and service commitment forms

As the *Transformed Giving* campaign comes to a close, members of the congregation should find themselves ready and willing to enter new levels of commitment in a variety of areas. That's where the commitment cards and service commitment forms come in. Sample copies are included on the CD-ROM toolkit, but it will be necessary to tailor the service commitment forms to include areas of service specific to your church family.

The commitment cards and service commitment forms will be mailed to church members individually a few weeks before the campaign ends. This allows enough time to give proper thought and prayer to their response.

It's important that no member of the congregation be surprised by the introduction of these documents. Throughout the campaign, the church family will be preparing for new levels of commitment, so the receipt of these items comes simply as the next step in the process. The entire study is based on a heart change, rather than strong-arm tactics. By Commitment Sunday, members should commit out of a desire to serve God, to grow closer to him, and to participate in the work he's doing, rather than feeling like it's something that they have to do.

That said, each member should be strongly encouraged to sign a commitment card and service commitment form for all areas—prayers, presence, gifts, and service—no matter what that commitment is. Encourage members to take part immediately, so they don't miss the opportunity for God's blessings and so they can experience the fullness of heart that comes with venturing into deeper levels of faithfulness.

As for what's actually on the cards, that will vary depending on the congregation. It's important, though, that the cards incorporate all elements of the study: prayer, presence, gifts, and service. There may be a listing of various opportunities for serving, blank lines that allow people to commit to a certain amount of money per week or month, and a section that commits support through prayer and attendance. Don't forget to include a place for each member to actually sign his or her name, giving added credence to the commitment. Some examples of commitment cards and service commitment forms are provided on the CD-ROM toolkit and are shown in the appendix.

For those who attend but don't turn in a card, a letter can be sent to their home. A sample of such a letter is provided on the CD-ROM toolkit and is shown in the appendix.

The actual giving back of a completed commitment card and service commitment form on Commitment Sunday should be done in a spirit of reverent celebration. It can be a moving, beautiful experience to see every person or family in a worship service come up to the front of the church to reverently and publicly give their commitment to the church by placing their cards and forms in a basket.

To make the moment even more special, you might consider giving a commemorative gift to each family or individual that turns in a commitment card and service commitment form. Such gifts don't need to be expensive, but communicate that their offering is valued. Since Commitment Sunday frequently comes right before Thanksgiving, your church might want to give a special Christmas tree ornament imprinted with the campaign logo and/or your church name. Other gift examples might be mugs, umbrellas, pens, keychains, or other personalized gifts. If you choose to thank your members with a gift, these could be handed to people when they deliver their commitment cards and service commitment forms during worship.

prayer

If there's only one thing you remember from this entire campaign handbook, let this be it: *God must remain an essential part of everything you do. He is ready and willing to offer insight and help wherever it's needed.*

To help things run as smoothly as possible—and to give members of the church family an opportunity to stretch in their own prayer lives—*Transformed Giving* has a prayer element built right in. Your church might establish a schedule of volunteers to pray continuously throughout the forty-day period. The beauty of it is that once it's set in place, you might find a core group willing to continue it long after the campaign has finished.

You might also consider organizing a vigil for the last twenty-four hours prior to Commitment Sunday. This can be a great time of worship and praising God for all that's he done and all he's yet to do. Additionally, you may want to consider holding a leadership prayer dinner about a week before the campaign kicks off. That can help build excitement, as well as express gratitude for those who have led the way thus far.

decisions to be made

Transformed Giving can be adapted for literally any church, whether big or small. Depending on the church structure, budget, and goals, however, some decisions will need to be made about how the study is actually implemented. The following questions should be addressed by the pastor, stewardship committee, and possibly other church leadership before the study begins.

1. **How should a date be determined for Commitment Sunday?**

   If you have a day that's traditionally set aside for a Commitment Sunday, this will be an easy substitution. Many churches already have an annual stewardship campaign each fall to help support the budget for the following year.

   If you don't already have a date in mind, autumn is a good time for many reasons. The main one is that we have all been programmed to expect autumn as a time of new beginnings. As we were growing up, there were always new school years, new semesters, new school clothes, and new friends to look forward to each fall. As such, we innately understand that this season is one for something new, and it's the season for learning.

   There's one caveat, however: If you're setting an autumn date for your Commitment Sunday, don't wait so late that you get close to the Christmas season. You don't want people to miss weekly events due to holiday obligations, plus you want people to establish their new habits of increased giving, service, and prayer before extra holiday outings and responsibilities distract them. The Sunday prior to Thanksgiving, then, could be an ideal time. John Ed Mathison would tell you that this date has worked well at his church.

2. **Who pays for the books?**

   Personal reading of *Treasures of the Transformed Life* is an essential part of the study for the congregation. Without the books, the campaign becomes nothing more than a series of messages from the pastor. You must decide, however, who will cover the cost.

   - Will the church purchase the books in advance, and then ask members of the church family to reimburse the church when they pick them up? (This will be the most common approach.)

- Will the church cover the cost of the books to distribute to the congregation for free?

- Or will the solution fall somewhere in between, with the church picking up part of the cost and offering the books to the congregation at a discounted rate?

The answer depends entirely on your congregation. Low-income families, for example, may see the cost of the book as prohibitive. You want to be careful that people aren't left out if they can't afford to purchase one. If the books are sold to members of the congregation at full or reduced costs, consider a special appeal, asking members of the church family if they'd be willing to sponsor someone in need by adding in a little extra cash.

3. How will the books/workbooks be distributed?

Copies of *Treasures of the Transformed Life* and *Participant's Workbook* should be available on Sunday mornings before and after worship services. To keep a close eye on the number distributed, they could be picked up at a table in the church narthex. Have church members initial or sign to be sure people have received copies and to keep track of inventory.

The books are intended for individual study, but one copy per family should work just fine (sharing can be good!). The associated *Participant's Workbook*, however, should be available per person, since there's journaling space and places to fill in the blanks and take notes. Remember to include sufficient copies for teens and older children when figuring out how many workbooks to order.

Throughout the campaign, it will be a good idea to keep extra copies at the church office so those who missed the original distribution won't be penalized. If your church office does not keep regular hours during the week, appoint someone as a contact for materials, making sure that person's phone number is listed in conjunction with church bulletin inserts, newsletter columns, and the like for anyone who decides to join in.

4. **Will your church use the provided program theme and graphics, or will you design your own?**

The answer to this depends entirely on the creativity, skill, and time available for planning. You've been provided with everything you need, but if there's enough time and interest within the stewardship committee, feel free to make it your own.

Whatever you decide, remember to be consistent. A graphic like the provided pearl and oyster—if repeated on newsletter columns, bulletin inserts, posters, and banners—can help instill the idea that the study reaches all members of the church and touches all church programs.

Giving wearable stickers with the campaign logo to every person at worship each week of the study can also reinforce the theme and unity. Stickers aren't expensive and are disposable, but entering church on Sunday and seeing everyone wearing the same lapel sticker helps create an atmosphere that says we're all together and this is a special season.

5. **What are the additional program expenses?**

Don't forget to factor in incidental costs such as printing, postage, the creation of signs and banners, or refreshments for Commitment Sunday. Discuss beforehand where the money will come from in the church's budget. Consider whether you want to reinforce the unified theme by passing out campaign stickers at all services and if you want to give thank-you gifts.

incorporating the church web site

One of the most important aspects of *Transformed Giving* is that it's a program the entire church can experience together. The reality, however, is that someone is bound to miss an occasional group meeting. Maybe someone serving with the children doesn't get a chance to attend Sunday school. Maybe someone who's sick or homebound misses out on one of the pastor's sermons. Maybe someone else with a third-shift work schedule is finding it hard to link up with others for community discussions.

The answer to this situation could come through technology. An increasing number of churches have Web sites. Some are even incorporating regularly updated components that appeal to those who might otherwise be out of touch. Digital availability is also high on the priority list for many teens and young adults, who increasingly receive information and insight through the Internet.

If your church already has a Web site, consider incorporating *Treasures of the Transformed Life* as a component. You might post a key question or two from the individual lessons of the *Participant's Workbook* to *Treasures of the Transformed Life* during the week after each meeting takes place. For an interactive experience, consider including some of the workbook's fill-in-the-blank questions.

If you'd like to take it a step further, your church's Web site could incorporate a blog or commentary section through which people could post their own thoughts or respond to those of others. One of the most exciting things about that approach is that people outside the church walls would also have access to view the comments. People who might be hesitant to set foot inside the actual church building would still be able to take part in intriguing dialogue about important spiritual topics. If you decide to go this route, however, it's important to appoint a Web moderator who can make sure comments stay on track.

Another option is to post the pastor's sermons (either portions or the entire messages) on the Web site as text, audio files, or even video files. Reinforcing the campaign in a Web format could be a good kicking-off point for incorporating more multimedia into your church programs. The CD-ROM toolkit has JPEG files of the graphics, as well as the contents of the newsletter articles and bulletin inserts.

Other ideas for Web site content include:

- a sample commitment card and service commitment form showing the variety of places where people can plug into the church;

- a reminder of the Scripture verse for each week;

- a countdown ticker to Commitment Sunday to build excitement; and

- previews of the coming week's message.

adapting for youth and families

You might think that *Transformed Giving* is only a program for the church's adults. But that's not necessarily so; *Treasures of the Transformed Life* and its workbook are both at a level that could be easily understood by teens. Consider involving your church's youth leadership as soon as possible so they can incorporate the program into their own activities. Youth participation in servant activities, prayer, attendance, and financial gifts could be increased by incorporating teen-specific elements into the study.

Consider, for example, developing separate commitment cards and service commitment forms for youth (sample cards are included on the CD-ROM toolkit). These could include servant opportunities that have to do with youth events or with general church activities, showing teens how to find places to give of themselves. You may want to consider incorporating the taking of tithes and offerings into youth activities. Provide opportunities for teens to share input into where money could be spent to improve youth programs, and help them see that their own financial gifts could help those things happen.

On a more individual level, as teens go through the program with their own peers, they'll also have a shared experience and point of conversation with their parents. Families should be encouraged to talk about the various topics of *Treasures of the Transformed Life* with each other, opening up discussions on prayer, giving, service, and the like.

Engaging in family discussions doesn't just apply to teens. It's never too early to begin teaching children such biblical concepts as giving back to God and putting others before yourself. Children learn great things by seeing their parents actively model prayer, tithing, service, and regular church attendance.

the before and after

Each of us has our own idea of success, and that's true even when it comes to a campaign like *Transformed Giving*. Before you dive in, then, it's important to give some thought and prayer to what kind of results you'd like to see before it's all over.

As you consider the results you'd like to see, think about how the campaign might impact your church long-term. Think about what can be done to facilitate future growth and development. Discuss how people can be regularly reminded of the things they've learned and the new goals they've set. Consider if there's a way to incorporate Sunday school/small group accountability.

And be sure to determine how the service commitments will be followed up on by leadership to ensure that all members who volunteer are used in their appropriate areas of ministry.

And this isn't just an individual thing. It might not be a bad idea to bring it up during the first meeting of the stewardship committee. Have everyone take out a piece of paper and write down, say, three goals for discussion. The goals don't necessarily have to be shared with the entire congregation. They could simply be discussed among the members of the committee, helping define the purpose of the campaign.

Now, when it comes to those goals, it's important to be as specific as possible. It's easy to say, "I'd like to see greater unity among the congregation," but that's not really measurable. Instead, consider something like, "increase attendance in weekly Sunday school classes by 25 percent," "have at least 75 percent of members involved in specific ministries or service," or "secure $200,000 in commitments for the church's building project."

Your goals might seem lofty, but again, if the goals are set through prayer and communion with God, who says they can't be met? It's so important that we give God room to work.

And to help keep things in perspective, it's a good idea to take inventory before the program begins so you can compare the status of the church after the campaign ends. For example, take note of the following:

- average attendance for Sunday morning worship

- average attendance for Sunday school/small group meetings

- attendance figures as percentage of overall membership

- number of church members

- average amount given in tithes and offerings per person each week

- percentage of church membership actively involved in one or more areas of service

- current church budget

- current financial commitments for growth, development, or building campaigns

- number of ministries with unmet financial or staffing needs

As you can see, there are many ways a study like *Treasures of the Transformed Life* could offer measurable results. That's important for a variety of reasons. First, it ensures you a return on your investment, so you'll know whether your time and efforts were worthwhile when you consider another such endeavor. Second, it can build great faith to see God move in ways that only he can, and bring results in ways that only he will. And finally, should you choose to share some of these results with the entire congregation, they'll also get a lift in their faith level.

Those involved will have an opportunity to see how their individual efforts are part of the greater good and how effective a team can be when it works together. In addition, marked levels of success establish a new culture in the church, one in which every member is committed, involved, and enthusiastic about continuing the new norms. It's built-in accountability so the church doesn't fall back on its old habits once the campaign is through.

chapter 6
components of the campaign

his program kit contains the key components you need to carry out a *Transformed Giving* campaign in your church. Each element of the campaign was briefly mentioned in the first chapter of this handbook, but here's a closer look:

- *Campaign Handbook.* This handbook serves as your roadmap, checklist, strategy plan, and communication material source for the entire campaign. It explains the campaign, defines the how-tos, lays out a chronology for tasks, and includes samples of materials you can create or use as they are.

- *Treasures of the Transformed Life: Satisfying Your Soul's Thirst for More.* This book by John Ed Mathison uses the theme of water to help readers dive in to the depths that God has for them. It helps participants recognize their thirst for more of God in their lives.

Step by step, it then explains how to satisfy that thirst through a dynamic prayer life, servant opportunities, selfless giving, and becoming an active member of the church team. The book is broken into forty separate lessons, with a review at the end of each week. Each day's lesson offers an opportunity for readers to prayerfully answer a handful of introspective questions, thereby deepening the experience.

- *Participant's Workbook* to *Treasures of the Transformed Life.* The workbook is meant to be used alongside the book, and includes space for individual journaling. It's also intended for use in small group/Sunday school classes. The workbook includes six weekly lessons, complete with fill-in-the-blank components and questions for group discussion.

- *Leader's Guide.* The *Leader's Guide* has all the same information as the *Participant's Workbook*, but also includes a DVD with six video introductions from John Ed Mathison. It also offers strategic help and encouragement for small group leaders who will facilitate the study.

- Campaign Media Kit
  - CD-ROM Toolkit
    - *Sample sermons:* During the forty-day studies at his own church, Mathison presents sermons related to the previous week's readings, bringing home the message in an assembly setting. He's done the same with *Treasures of the Transformed Life,* and you can look to his sermons for ideas and inspiration.

    - *Bulletin inserts*: The more a message is repeated, the more likely it is to stick. As such, in addition to interrelated daily readings, weekly small group meetings, and Sunday sermons, church members can find a brief summary—and also a look ahead—in the church bulletin. You'll find examples of the eight inserts in the appendix of this book. Those inserts are also included on the CD-ROM toolkit.

– *Newsletter columns*: Since so many churches offer mid-week newsletters, this is a way to keep up enthusiasm on the days away from the church building. These columns are found in the appendix and also ready to go on the CD-ROM toolkit. Each column will offer a reminder to keep up with the week's daily readings, so church members won't miss out on all of the great things going on.

– *Sample service commitment forms*: Service commitment is crucial to the lifeblood of the church and the spiritual growth of members. Having a method people use to volunteer for and commit to areas of service is just as critical. Included are two modifiable versions (in Microsoft® Word) of service commitment forms that your church can use to assist in this indispensable area.

– *Poster, pledge cards, supplemental letters, graphics, etc.*: Feel free to use the ones provided or to develop your own.

- DVDs
  – *Weekly introductions*: Each small group meeting/Sunday school gathering during the forty-day period will integrate the *Treasures of*

the Transformed Life study. To help set the tone
for those meetings, the facilitator will begin by
playing a brief introductory DVD segment. The
six messages, one for each week, offer a personal
touch to each topic, as well as a level of consistency to each lesson.

– *Messages for Pastor and Committee:* Nobody
says it like John Ed Mathison, and these components of *Transformed Giving* offer an
opportunity to hear straight from his heart. First,
there's the explanatory message for the church
pastor. It's a heart-to-heart, pastor-to-pastor talk
on money, commitment, courage, and the how-tos
of pulling together a stewardship committee that
can take the church to the next level.

There's also a motivational message for the
stewardship committee, once it's in place. It
covers personal responsibility, giving God room
to work, and insight on how giving can be seen as
an opportunity rather than a necessity.

Finally, *Transformed Giving* includes a brief
message for pastors and other church leaders
that discusses the ins and outs of personal testimonies. According to Mathison, personal
testimonies allow members of the church family
to hear from their peers how God is moving
among them, but they also solidify the life-
changing experiences for the person doing the
talking. The DVD includes real-life examples of
testimony interviews.

ministry by
the people

A bove all else, it's important to remember that *Transformed Giving* isn't just about money. Certainly, that's a big part of it. But the goal here is not just to have people release more from their checkbooks; it is to help them release more of themselves. In addition to financial gifts, service is an aspect of the Christian walk that is too powerful to be ignored. This campaign can help members of the congregation understand that by giving of their time and talents, they can walk more closely with God and can better understand his purposes for their lives.

So how do you get them involved? Mathison's church focuses on service based on the concept of volunteerism. Rather than arm-twisting or manipulation, they make volunteering mean-ingful, fun, and exciting—and that attitude is contagious. When lay members witness about specific ministries they're involved in and what that involvement has meant to their lives, others start thinking about areas in which they can volunteer, as well.

Treasures of the Transformed Life goes into detail about discovering gifts and talents and finding places to serve, and we'll go over some of that here. But first, understand that the impetus for service must come straight from leadership. Rather than something that's simply hoped for, commitment to volunteerism and service shows that being involved is an expected part of church life, just like showing up on Sunday mornings. It's not something that's mentioned once and then forgotten; it needs to be reiterated again and again, echoed from the pulpit, the Sunday school classrooms, and person to person.

serving is belonging

When people join an organization, church or otherwise, their level of commitment has a lot to do with the level of expectation they find. As such, when people join your church, they should be given an opportunity right away to say where they feel called to serve. That will help them feel like they belong.

That can be a quite different scenario from one in which people have to wait to be asked to do anything. Those who are new or not well known may fall through the cracks, while the people who already do a lot may continuously be asked to keep doing more. Aside from all that, trying to figure out who would be good at what task can add up to a tremendous waste of time for the church leadership.

Volunteering is always better than being recruited. Keep in mind that most people are uncomfortable saying no to the pastor. If the pastor (or someone else in leadership) asks someone to be involved in a certain area of ministry, that person may say yes even if they really have no interest in serving there. That can lead to problems in the long run, as well as a general lack of enthusiasm—and therefore, effectiveness—along the way.

Because he has seen it work with his church's own program, Mathison considers the volunteering and involvement of all church members in service to be the most powerful method of transforming congregations and developing deep commitment. Get people involved and they change in many areas, including financial giving. So even though soliciting volunteers during the course of your stewardship campaign may seem like extra work, it's important. Your church will have far better results if it embraces and implements the service commitment part of the *Transformed Giving* program.

service made easy

If your church already has a structure in place for identifying service needs and soliciting volunteer workers, consider the following ideas simply as new ways to keep your volunteer recruitment fresh. If your church doesn't have a systematic method of linking service needs with volunteers, the *Transformed Giving* program makes it simple.

Begin with identifying service needs by meeting with lay leaders and staff to solicit a list of service opportunities. Make the list as complete as possible; consider things as large as finding someone who will overhaul your Web site to needs as small as vacuuming the carpet in the church. Look for ongoing needs, such as ushering on a weekly basis as well as one-time-only services, like mulching church flower beds in the fall.

Once you have a comprehensive list, you'll be ready to develop your own service commitment forms. The CD-ROM toolkit has a sample template in Microsoft Word of the form shown in the appendix. This document can be easily modified to accommodate the specific ministries in your congregation. (This particular commitment form was based on one developed and used successfully by a small-membership congregation, and it's patterned after the model used by Mathison's church.)

Send the commitment card and service commitment form to each church member by mail, noting it is to be returned on Commitment Sunday.

After members have turned in their service commitment forms, have someone go through them all and compile the responses and areas of service. Some churches use computer software programs to track volunteers and the areas of service in which they volunteered.

It's really important that the person in charge of the service area diligently follows up on the volunteer responses. There is perhaps nothing more demoralizing to someone who has volunteered than to not be contacted to serve. Make it a goal to contact each new volunteer within two weeks of receiving the service commitment form. Equally important is to have each new volunteer begin service as soon as feasible, reinforcing the fact that volunteers are both needed and valued.

[The principles of implementing a volunteer culture are fully developed in John Ed Mathison's book, *Every Member in Ministry*, which is available by contacting Frazer Memorial. The church also offers conferences twice a year for churches that want to learn more about the Every Member in Ministry program. For further information, visit their Web site at www. frazerumc.org.]

releasing authority to volunteer laity

Now, when you open the door for people to volunteer, you might have people offering themselves in areas you wouldn't have expected. And they may not be the people you would have picked for the job. Occasionally, church staff and leadership can feel a little intimidated by the laity. There can be a fear of losing control as responsibilities are handed off to people who aren't on staff. But when members of the laity are released to grow in their giftings, wonderful things can happen. The congregation as a whole becomes more vibrant, committed, and involved. Energy and excitement become tangible, and with more hands on deck, the church is able to greatly expand its offerings to both its members and the outside community.

With a volunteer emphasis, the pastor may not know every-thing that the laity is doing, but that's not necessarily a bad thing. Mathison says that if a pastor knows everything going on in the church, there's not enough going on. Instead of a frustra-tion, this can actually be a freedom for the pastor who helps his congregation realize that everyone is in it together. It also allows the pastor to focus on the things that only the pastor can do, and to release the rest to others.

Since ministry is initiated by God, allowing people to volun-teer for areas of service—and encouraging them to grow in those areas of service—helps them learn to make effective deci-sions with God's guidance, and to grow in their ability to walk with him and hear him. Of course, training can and should be offered in various areas of ministry, but at the same time, allow room for creativity.

each member—and each ministry— is important

If we truly believe that we're the body of Christ—and that every part of that body is important for it to function as a whole—then every member of the church must have some vital role to play. Now, not every person will be gifted in the area of leading worship, teaching Sunday school, or singing in the choir. But each person brings something to the table, and by helping people find what their gifting is, you can help them grow in confidence and maturity.

Keep in mind that a task one person has no interest in doing could be an absolute delight for someone else. It doesn't really matter if the task is large or small, as long as it's done in love. One person might like to write letters to new members or people in times of need, for example. Another might make sure the pew racks are stocked with appropriate materials and sharpened pencils. Another might want to develop the church Web site. And yet another may be willing to stand in the parking lot and help people into the church building as needed. Each task can have a significant impact on both the congregation and the person who volunteers to do it.

No doubt, as your church moves to an understanding that everyone is expected to be involved, there will be members who feel they have nothing to offer. There's more information about discovering particular gifts and talents in *Treasures of the Transformed Life*. But if members of the congregation really struggle with the issue, try a few exercises. Ask them what they're passionate about, and what they're doing when they feel the most joy or peace. Ask them where they have particular skills or interests, and look for creative ways that those can be plugged into ministry areas at the church. And finally, ask them to pray for direction. God may lead them to a particular area of service that they may not have imagined for themselves, and by being encouraged to step out and take part, they can better walk in his will.

Of course, each church will have its own set of needs and opportunities for service, and it will be up to your church's leadership and ministry leaders to determine what might be listed on your church's service commitment form. There are some generic categories that most congregations are involved in, such as teaching Sunday school, working in the nursery, ushering, participating in music/choir, assisting with office administration, working with the youth, and helping with the food ministry. As such, we've included a service commitment form that can help you get started, as well as a couple of actual examples from churches.

Pray it through, though, and prepare to see God raise up unlikely leaders in your midst.

chapter 8

campaign chronology

E ven though *Treasures of the Transformed Life* is billed as a forty-day, or six-week, study, the planning must begin before that. Ideally, the clock starts ticking several months before the campaign begins, allowing enough time to effectively delegate tasks. This will also allow time for excitement and momentum to build within the church, rather than forcing a last-minute, rushed effort that doesn't come across as important or well planned.

If you've just received this study and there are fewer than three months until your church's annual stewardship campaign, don't panic. Just do the best you can, consolidating steps as necessary. God will work with you no matter where you are.

three months before kickoff

_____ pastor watches *Transformed Giving WILL Transform Your Church* introductory DVD segment

_____ pastor appoints chair of stewardship committee, if no such committee is in place

_____ pastor and committee chair read *Treasures of the Transformed Life* book

_____ stewardship committee job descriptions are reviewed and accepted by lay leadership

two months before kickoff

_____ chair of stewardship committee, with the help of the pastor, appoints committee members

_____ stewardship committee holds its first meeting and watches *Transformed Giving as a Group Effort* DVD segment; pastor meets with committee to encourage full participation

_____ sample copies of *Treasures of the Transformed Life* are ordered for committee members

_____ program graphics and printing strategies are determined and initiated

_____ work on the service commitment form begins, with church leadership determining areas of service needs

_____ optional program features such as providing thank-you gifts or sticker giveaways are discussed and committee decides if they'll be implemented

six weeks before kickoff

_____ stewardship committee holds second meeting after sample copies arrive; the books are then distributed to committee members

_____ roles are delegated during the meeting

    _____ book distribution coordinator

    _____ small group coordinator

    _____ volunteer commitment coordinator

    _____ communications coordinator

    _____ print resources coordinator

    _____ prayer coordinator

_____ testimony coordinator
_____ follow-up coordinator
_____ comparative study coordinator
_____ hospitality coordinator

one month before kickoff

_____ stewardship committee meets to discuss progress in each delegated task

_____ books, workbooks, and Sunday school/small group *Leader's Guides* with DVD are ordered for the congregation (see Cokesbury ordering information enclosed with *Transformed Giving* program kit)

_____ statistics are gathered for pre- and post-campaign comparison, such as average Sunday attendance, average amount of tithe, etc. This continues weekly through end of campaign

_____ Sunday school/small group leader recruitment begins (if not already in place in your body)

_____ church Webmaster is contacted about including online elements of study during the campaign

_____ youth leaders are contacted to discuss incorporation of youth activities in regard to the campaign

_____ posters/banners/etc. are displayed in church announcing an upcoming event

_____ letter from pastor or stewardship committee chair mailed to congregation to introduce the campaign

_____ arrangements made for a leadership prayer dinner to be held one week before kickoff

two weeks before kickoff

_____ church newsletter and bulletin are prepared and printed for distribution the following week

_____ copies of *Treasures of the Transformed Life* and the *Participant's Workbook* are made available to congregation

_____ recruitment of Sunday school/small group leaders
continues

_____ *Leader's Guide* distributed to Sunday school/small
group leaders

one week before kickoff

_____ first columns appear in church newsletter and bulletin

_____ ensure Sunday school/small group leaders have all necessary materials to begin the campaign the following week

_____ complete design of commitment card and service
commitment form, including areas of service, prayer,
attendance, and financial commitments, and take to
printer or make arrangements for duplication

_____ first witness is secured to give testimony about the study
during the following week's worship service, with a focus
on God's commitment to us and our commitment to him

_____ copies of *Treasures of the Transformed Life* and the
Participant's Workbook are made available to congregation members who have not yet received one

_____ recruitment of Sunday school/small group leaders ends;
Leader's Guide distributed to any leaders who haven't
yet received copies

_____ hold leadership prayer dinner

kickoff week

_____ copies of *Treasures of the Transformed Life* and the
Participant's Workbook are made available to congregation members who have not yet received one

_____ second columns appear in church newsletter and bulletin

_____ pastor gives brief introduction to the study and encourages church members to begin the daily readings of
Treasures of the Transformed Life in the coming week

_____ if the small group studies will be held during mid-week
meetings, those meetings take place this week

_____ congregation begins daily readings of *Treasures of the Transformed Life*

first week of the campaign

_____ congregation continues daily readings of *Treasures of the Transformed Life*

_____ third columns appear in church newsletter and bulletin

_____ campaign theme stickers are passed out as members enter church on Sunday (optional)

_____ on Sunday, pastor gives sermon related to part I of *Treasures of the Transformed Life*, "Priming the Pump"

_____ during worship service, first witness gives testimony related to part I of *Treasures of the Transformed Life*

_____ Sunday school/small groups watch first DVD segment and discuss part I of *Treasures of the Transformed Life*

_____ second witness is secured to give testimony about prayer during the following week's assembly

second week of the campaign

_____ congregation continues daily readings of *Treasures of the Transformed Life*

_____ fourth columns appear in church newsletter and bulletin

_____ campaign stickers are passed out as members enter church on Sunday (optional)

_____ on Sunday, pastor gives sermon related to part II of *Treasures of the Transformed Life*, "Drawing Water"

_____ during worship service, second witness gives testimony related to part II of *Treasures of the Transformed Life*

_____ Sunday school/small groups watch second DVD segment and discuss part II of *Treasures of the Transformed Life*

_____ third witness is secured to give testimony with a focus on presence

_____ commitment cards and service commitment forms are prepared for mailing the following week

third week of the campaign

_____ congregation continues daily readings of *Treasures of the Transformed Life*

_____ fifth columns appear in church newsletter and bulletin

_____ stewardship committee meets to discuss progress of campaign and discuss ideas in more detail for continuing the momentum once the campaign ends

_____ campaign theme stickers are passed out as members enter church on Sunday (optional)

_____ pastor gives sermon on Sunday related to part III of *Treasures of the Transformed Life*, "Jumping In with Both Feet"

_____ Sunday school/small groups watch third DVD segment and discuss part III of *Treasures of the Transformed Life*

_____ during worship service, third witness gives testimony with a focus on presence

_____ letter from the pastor or stewardship committee chair (or jointly from both) is sent to the congregation on Monday, encouraging continued participation in the study; commitment cards and service commitment forms to be turned in on Commitment Sunday are included in the mailing

_____ fourth witness is secured to give testimony about the study during the following week's assembly, with a focus on financial gifts

fourth week of the campaign

_____ congregation continues daily readings of *Treasures of the Transformed Life*

_____ sixth columns appear in church newsletter and bulletin

_____ campaign theme stickers are passed out as members enter church on Sunday (optional)

_____ pastor gives sermon on Sunday related to part IV of *Treasures of the Transformed Life*, "Pennies in the Fountain"

during worship service, fourth witness gives testimony
with a focus on financial gifts related to part IV of
Treasures of the Transformed Life

Sunday school/small groups watch fourth DVD segment
and discuss part IV of *Treasures of the Transformed Life*

fifth witness is secured to give testimony about service

fifth week of the campaign

congregation continues daily readings of *Treasures of
the Transformed Life*

seventh columns appear in church newsletter and bulletin

campaign theme stickers are passed out as members
enter church on Sunday (optional)

pastor gives sermon on Sunday related to part V of
Treasures of the Transformed Life, "Offering a Drink
to Others"

during worship service, fifth witness gives testimony
focusing on service

Sunday school/small groups watch fifth DVD segment
and discuss part V of *Treasures of the Transformed Life*

sixth witness is secured to give testimony about the study
during the Commitment Sunday assembly, with a focus
on continuing to grow in our relationship with God

leadership meal is held for stewardship committee and
other church leaders who have been key to implementing
campaign

commitment sunday

congregation has completed daily readings of *Treasures of
the Transformed Life*

eighth column appears in church bulletin

Sunday school/small groups watch sixth DVD segment
and discuss part VI of *Treasures of the Transformed Life*

_____ campaign theme stickers are passed out as members enter
church on Sunday (optional)

_____ pastor gives sermon on Sunday related to part VI of
Treasures of the Transformed Life, "Filling the Bucket to
Overflowing"

_____ during worship service, sixth witness gives testimony
related to continuing to grow in our relationship with God

_____ commitment cards and service commitment forms are
turned in during worship service

_____ communion held during worship service

_____ thank-you gifts given to members turning in forms (optional)

week following commitment sunday

_____ commitment cards and service commitment forms are
distributed to appropriate leadership for follow-up

_____ follow-up letters, commitment cards, and service commitment forms are sent to those who have not yet responded

_____ thank-you letters are sent to those who turned in commitment cards and service commitment forms

_____ final statistics are gathered for post-campaign comparison

_____ eighth column appears in newsletter

two weeks after commitment sunday

_____ stewardship committee meets to go over pre- and post-
campaign comparison

_____ formal report is prepared for pastor, including what worked
best during the study, what didn't, and what can be done in
the future to make similar campaigns even more effective

materials used in
the campaign

T his appendix contains a number of resources that may be used to help spread the word about your church's *Transformed Giving* campaign. Many of them are designed to be used as they are by copying directly from the CD-ROM toolkit, and others might only need a church letterhead or name attached to the copy. All resources are formatted as Microsoft Word files or Adobe® Acrobat® (.pdf) files.

11 x 17 color poster.
Adobe PDF graphic file available
on CD-ROM toolkit.

1-color, standard letterhead and envelope.
Modifiable text in MS Word
available on CD-ROM toolkit.

Dear family member:

Exciting days are ahead.

We're about to introduce a life-changing opportunity for our church family, and it's a chance for us to dive deeper into all that God has for us, both individually and as a congregation.

In coming weeks, you'll be able to pick up a copy of *Treasures of the Transformed Life: Satisfying Your Soul's Thirst for More* immediately before or after the worship service. This book includes forty daily readings that will challenge you in the areas of service, prayer, attendance, financial gifts, and commitment. You'll have the chance to ask yourself some probing questions about what you believe and why. Please take advantage of all that this book has to offer. Set aside a few brief moments for introspection each day, and I guarantee that the Lord will meet you exactly where you are. He'll begin to fulfill desires of your heart that you might not even realize you have.

To deepen your experience, we'll be discussing each week's topics in both our small group/Sunday school meetings and in worship. That way, we'll all have the opportunity to grow as one, reaching for a common goal—a rich, rewarding, blessed life of adventure, joy, peace, and purpose.

At the end of the study, we'll all take part in Commitment Sunday, when we'll have a chance to put our faith into action. That will be here soon enough. For now, let's focus on the task at hand.

Do your best to attend worship services in the coming weeks, and keep your eye out for the start of the campaign. I'd hate for you to miss a moment as we all embark on this journey together. And please, join me in prayer that God would indeed "throw open the floodgates of heaven," as he promises in Malachi 3:10 (NIV), and pour out so much blessing individually and corporately that we don't have room to contain it.

There's so much more to God than we can even imagine. During the course of this forty-day study, however, we'll have an opportunity to see him and his presence in our lives in an entirely new way.

Sincerely,

Dear family member:

What an incredible ride it's been.

Hard to believe, but our *Treasures of the Transformed Life* study is quickly passing by. Commitment Sunday is just a few weeks away.

At this point, I'd like you to think back over some of the key concepts from the study and recall your Scripture verses. I want you to think back to the beginning and what your expectations were. Did God meet you there? Have you found new levels of thirst and new ways of satisfying that thirst? How is God continuing to deepen your levels of trust, faith, and wisdom as you continue your daily readings?

Personally, I believe this study is bringing us closer as a congregation, and truly establishing the idea that the church is family. I'm excited to see how these new levels of unity will make us even more effective in showing Christ to our community. I'm excited, too, about new levels of commitment through service, prayer, and financial gifts.

But we can't keep taking it all in without giving anything back. So now's the time to put your faith into action. There's a commitment card and service commitment form for each family member enclosed with this letter, and I'd like you to begin thinking about how you'll fill them out, so they will be ready to turn in on Commitment Sunday. As you'll notice, you have the opportunity to be specific about which areas of service you'd like to take part in, and how much you plan to give financially. Do remember that the more you're willing to share in terms of time, money, and effort, the more opportunity you give the Lord to bless you in return. The life poured out, after all, is the one that God can more easily fill.

I'd like to remind you to consider your commitments with much prayer. God wants to partner with you in his work, and involving him in the decision-making process ensures that his will is done, rather than simply our own.

I do hope this experience has been a rich, rewarding one for you, and I'd like encourage you to continue any good habits in regard to prayer, Bible study, community, or group discussion you're picking up along the way. This is by no means an end. Rather, it's a beginning to a new life that God has called us to, one that we can enjoy both as individuals and as part of the church family.

See you on Sunday!

Sincerely,

Congregational letter #2.
Modifiable text available on CD-ROM toolkit.

Dear family member:

Good for you!

I've just received word that you turned in a commitment card and service commitment form during Commitment Sunday, and I'd like to personally thank you for taking the time and making the effort. May the Lord richly bless you in return!

This campaign has been such an incredible time for our church, but the truth is, there's no point in doing it without the enthusiasm and dedication of people like you. It is my hope and prayer that your experience with *Treasures of the Transformed Life* has been a rich one, and that the lessons learned would be ones that stay with you for the rest of your life.

As you move forward in your new commitments to prayers, presence, service, and financial gifts, keep in mind that the Lord will be by your side every step of the way. He will provide in ways you've yet to imagine, and watching him work is half the fun.

Thanks again for being a vital, irreplaceable part of our church family. You are loved.

Sincerely,

Dear family member:

We recently wrapped up our *Treasures of the Transformed Life* campaign, culminating with Commitment Sunday. It was an awesome opportunity for every member of the church to make a fresh commitment in regard to service, prayer, attendance, and financial gifts, as well as a chance for the church to move ahead as a unified team.

But as we've been going through the cards and forms that were turned in, we've noticed that there aren't any from you.

First of all, if you did indeed turn a card and form in and you've received this letter in error, please let the church office know. We're excited to help you begin serving as soon as possible.

If, for some reason, you never received a commitment card and service commitment form, it's not too late to turn them in. I've included copies with this letter so you can still take part. Simply drop these in the offering plate on Sunday.

You know, you can also use these if you've simply been undecided until now. If that's the case, I'd encourage you to take a small step of faith and remember that God will meet you wherever you are.

This study has been such a blessing for our entire church family, and I want to make sure that you don't miss out. Our body simply isn't complete without the gifts, talents, and presence you bring to the table. Won't you join us?

Sincerely,

Congregational letter #4.
Modifiable text available on CD-ROM toolkit.

transformed living

treasures *of the* **transformed life**

satisfying your soul's thirst for more

JOHN ED MATHISON

Ever heard the phrase "pearl of wisdom"? It implies a thought so precious and powerful that it's considered priceless. And you've got an entire string of them headed your way.

In coming weeks, this spot in the bulletin will be your anchor for *Treasures of the Transformed Life*, a churchwide event that will help you grow closer to God through a fresh understanding of prayer, church attendance, financial giving, and service. That event is loaded with insight that can take us from where we are to places we never imagined we could be.

But if you're going to get anything out of it, you're going to have to put something into it. You can start by picking up your own copy of *Treasures of the Transformed Life*, a forty-day study that will help you dive into the Bible and into God's presence. We'll all start reading the book after next Sunday, the kickoff day for the entire campaign.

You'll start discussing what you've learned in your Sunday school/small group meeting. Along the way, the pastor's messages will tie in to the weekly themes, too. But don't let the pastor do all the work. There's plenty to be learned in your own private times of prayer and introspection as you dive into the daily readings.

So get ready. The next couple of months could be a turning point in your life, a chance for you to pick up a string of priceless pearls and wear them for all to see. Pray expectantly, knowing that God will be faithful to meet you wherever you are.

See you right here next week!

transformed living

Pearl of Wisdom:
Don't be afraid to go out on a limb. That's where the fruit is.
—H. Jackson Brown

treasures
of the
transformed
life

satisfying your soul's thirst for more

JOHN ED MATHISON

Before you leave today, if you haven't already, be sure to pick up your copy of *Treasures of the Transformed Life*. It's a forty-day study that the entire church will be going through together, and you simply don't want to miss it. This is going to be a great opportunity to grow in faith and stretch your spirit.

So what should you expect? For starters, plan now to set aside a few extra minutes each day to go over the readings and prayerfully consider the topics presented. They're certain to speak straight to your heart.

But count on something else, too: being a part of the big picture as our entire congregation moves through the study together. We'll talk about the concepts in our Sunday school/small group meetings, and the pastor's messages will offer further insight each week. There's no telling how God can move among us when we're all on the same page—literally.

The study will finish with Commitment Sunday, a chance for you to dive into commitment and see what God will do in return. Now's the time to start fresh, to look ahead, and to be expectant that God will accomplish great things right here in our church body. What are you waiting for?

Coming up next week: The only way to truly satisfy your thirst.

Bulletin insert #2.
Adobe PDF graphic files available on CD-ROM toolkit.

transformed living

Pearl of Wisdom:

The life that God has for us, the one he really intends for us to live,
is a lot like a glass of pure water. It's refreshing, it's good for us,
and it satisfies our thirst in a way that absolutely nothing else can.

So how's that reading going? By now, you should have read through the first week of *Treasures of the Transformed Life*, the chapters on discovering your deep-down thirst and learning how to satisfy it.

Today's message will be on a related topic, so you'll have a chance to revisit, refresh, and renew what you've learned. Remember, for example, the story about the woman who tangled all her threads trying to do things on her own?

As you read through each chapter, don't forget to take a few minutes and prayerfully consider your answers to the Dive In questions. You might even make a few notes in the accompanying workbook. Remember: The more you put into this study, the more you'll get out of it in return.

So what is it you're drinking in this morning? Could you relate to the author's insights about trying to satisfy your thirst with anything you could get your hands on? Have you ever become complacent—or even bored—trying to live the good Christian life? How can that kind of life change to one that's vibrant and ever growing?

Coming up next week: Communication is a two-way street.

transformed living

Pearl of Wisdom:
When we pray consistently, we become like trees that are firmly planted, growing and producing much fruit.

At this point, you should be finished reading the second week of *Treasures of the Transformed Life*, the chapters on prayer. Are you ready to discuss the key points in your Sunday school/small group meeting? How did you feel, for example, about the author's insights on the bonsai and the sequoia? How deep are your own roots of prayer?

This morning, the pastor's message will cover a related topic, so you'll have the chance to revisit, refresh, and renew what you've learned. But you've got to remember that prayer is an individual thing. You can't grow in your own prayer life just by relying on the prayers of someone else.

So how long has it been since you've had a two-way conversation with God? How long has it been since you've asked for his advice or help? How long since you've admitted that you really can't handle everything on your own? It's not just that God needs to be needed, you know. It's that he wants us to remember that he is always there for us, willing to open his hand in our direction. So go ahead. Crawl up in your heavenly father's lap, and tell him about your day. He's certain to be all ears.

Coming up next week: We are family.

Bulletin insert #4.
Adobe PDF graphic files available on CD-ROM toolkit.

transformed living

Pearl of Wisdom:
*We've been picked for God's team, and we're all part of the
first draft. He wants each of us to be part of the family.*

And here we are at the end of the third week, halfway through *Treasures of the Transformed Life*. Are you finding any transformation in your own?

This week's readings covered the importance of presence. Remember how Woody Allen said, "Eighty percent of success is showing up"? Well, it's good that you're here—you've already succeeded! It's great that you understand the church needs you as much as you need it.

Take a minute to look around you and see all your brothers and sisters in God's family. Each one of them has passions, challenges, joys, and unanswered prayers, just like you. So how well do you know what they are? Before you leave today, connect with someone who's outside your normal circle. Offer a word of encouragement, a moment of prayer, or even a hand with a task. Along the way, you might notice an interesting thing happening: someone doing the same for you. Doesn't it feel great to love and be loved?

Since we're all part of God's family here on earth, we're called to love each other in a way that makes those on the outside want to join in. So what does your attitude towards others in your church family say to the world?

Coming up next week: What's in your wallet?

transformed living

Pearl of Wisdom:

What goes up must come down.
In the same way, the more we allow our financial gifts
to rise to the heavens through tithes and offerings,
the more likely we are to see abundant rain.

No one likes to talk about money. And you don't like anyone telling you what to do with it, either. But what if someone gave you some hard-earned insight on a solid investment, one with out-of-this-world rewards? Would you jump at the opportunity?

This week, your daily readings in *Treasures of the Transformed Life* looked at financial gifts. Remember the illustration of the water cycle, in which the moisture gathers on the ground, evaporates into the heavens, and then returns to the earth as precipitation? How's the precipitation in your own life?

As usual, the pastor's message will cover a related topic to help you revisit, refresh, and renew what you've learned. But that's not all. Just like every Sunday, the offering plate will be passed. Will you look at it with new eyes?

The way we feel about money, if you remember, says a lot about our priorities. And if we hold it in a clenched fist, rather than on an outstretched palm, a funny thing happens. It becomes all we have. A hand that's tightly closed has no way to receive.

So what's your posture toward giving this week? How tightly closed is that fist? How open is that heart?

Coming up next week: This church wants YOU!

Bulletin insert #6.
Adobe PDF graphic files available on CD-ROM toolkit.

transformed living

Pearl of Wisdom:
Many congregations find that they
have to recruit people for acts of service.
No telling how much time is wasted trying to
figure out who the best person might be for the job.
No telling how much more we could accomplish if
we weren't just sitting around, waiting to be asked.

If you're like many folks, you've heard your mother say, "I've asked you a thousand times." Maybe she was talking about picking up your laundry off the floor, not drinking out of the milk carton, or not leaving your bike parked in the driveway. Regardless, at some point, you stopped hearing her.

How would things have been different if just once you did what she wanted you to without her having to ask? Chances are, you both would have been much happier. She could have saved her breath, and you wouldn't have rolled your eyes.

This week's readings in *Treasures of the Transformed Life* were about service. The pastor's message will be about the same thing. So this morning, ask yourself a question: *Is there any place God has nudged me to serve that I haven't yet tried?*

If so, what are you waiting for? Someone else to ask you? Do yourself a favor: volunteer. The person on the receiving end will most likely be every bit as happy as your mother would have been the day she saw the bike in the garage rather than on the driveway.

Coming up next week: Sign on the dotted line.

transformed living

Pearl of Wisdom:
No longer can we say, "We didn't know."
We're accountable for what we've been taught.

Expecting a five-year-old to drive a car would be ridiculous. So would expecting a seven-year-old to cook a gourmet meal. See, those are skills that have to be taught. We don't come out of the womb knowing everything we need to know.

As we mature, however, we start seeing things in a new way. We overcome challenges, we gain new insight, and we grow.

Over the last six weeks, we've had a great opportunity to grow in a variety of ways. We've been shown new ways of looking at ourselves, at the world around us, and at God. And the time has come for us to demonstrate exactly what it is we've learned.

Today is Commitment Sunday, the final day of our churchwide study and our stewardship campaign. As a member of our church family, you've had a chance to the read the book, to discuss the concepts, and to hear the pastor's related messages. So what will your response be?

It's hoped you've prayerfully considered how to fill out your commitment card and service commitment form, and you're ready to turn them in. And if you never received them or you forgot to bring them today, don't worry; we have extras available for you to pick up today.

As you prepare to turn these commitments in, however, think back over the previous weeks. Consider your thirst. Think about your previous levels of commitment, and the new places you're stepping into today. And let the celebrations begin. It's a new day, after all, a new adventure, and a new life that's been transformed.

Bulletin insert #8.
Adobe PDF graphic files available on CD-ROM toolkit.

Are you satisfied with your life? Really satisfied?

It's often said that Christians have every reason in the world to be optimistic. We know that God is on our side, after all, and according to Romans 8:28, he's promised to work all things for our good because we love him.

And yet, if we were really honest about it, we'd admit that life can still be a challenge. Days can still seem ho-hum, rather than the awesome adventure we secretly long for.

Ever been there? Ever thirsted for more?

If so, here's the exciting news you've been waiting for: Our church family is about to embark on a forty-day study that can literally change the way you feel about prayer, church attendance, acts of service, and even financial giving. By the time it's all said and done, you'll be able to see your relationship with God in a whole new way, confidently understanding how to "live all the days of your life," per the well-known Irish blessing.

So where do you come in? First of all, know that the churchwide study will involve more than just a series of Sunday-morning sermons. You'll also read a book called *Treasures of the Transformed Life*, with forty days of lessons and insights that can help you define just what it is you're really thirsty for—and how to go about satisfying that thirst. You'll be given the opportunity to openly discuss what you're learning during weekly Sunday school/small group meetings, and you'll hear inspired messages each week to tie it all together.

We'll end the study together on Commitment Sunday, when you'll have a chance to put your faith into action.

Please don't miss this churchwide opportunity to grow in faith and stretch your spirit. Make plans now to attend this Sunday's worship service, so you can pick up your copy of *Treasures of the Transformed Life*.

And know that the transformed life that results could be your very own!

Feeling a little thirsty?

This past Sunday, we began distributing copies of John Ed Mathison's *Treasures of the Transformed Life*. The book is a forty-day study that shows us what we're really thirsty for—and how to satisfy that thirst. It is hoped by now you've started diving in.

You could go about this study one of several ways. First, you could ignore it. You could allow that book to gather dust on your nightstand table, and figure that you'll get the main points by hearing the pastor's sermons and listening to the discussions in Sunday school.

You could read the entire week's lessons in one sitting, maybe even on Saturday night or early Sunday morning. That way, you figure, you can catch up and still know what everybody is talking about.

Or you could set aside a little bit of time each day, going over the daily readings and prayerfully considering the answers to the probing questions. You could allow God to speak to both your heart and mind. You could openly discuss what you're learning in your small group, and you could gain from the insights of others as you find yourself sharing in humility, as well.

Really, the choice is yours. This isn't school, after all, with someone looking over your shoulder and grading you on your level of participation. No, this is between you and God.

You could look at this as simply one more thing to do in your already-busy schedule, or you could see it as the chance of a lifetime to press in and know God as you've never known him before.

E. Stanley Jones said once that, "Life in our hands is life on our hands—a problem. Life in the hands of Jesus is no longer a problem; it is a possibility."

So what's the greatest of possibilities today? Are you ready to dive in—even if it feels like you're in over your head—and allow God to help you swim?

Newsletter article #2.
Modifiable text available on CD-ROM toolkit.

If you've ever tried to drop a few pounds, you've probably noticed something interesting: You won't get very far if you only watch what you eat a couple of days a week, and you don't build much muscle if you only exercise once a month.

Prayer works the same way. You're not likely to notice much difference in your relationship with God if you only check in occasionally. You're not likely to build much faith if you're not regularly stretching your ears to hear.

This week's lesson from *Treasures of the Transformed Life* focuses on prayer. It's presented as the root system that helps us grow and flourish, much like the tree planted by the riverside, with constant access to living water.

Remember the week's Scripture verse, introduced in the Sunday school/small group lesson: "I am the vine; you are the branches. Those who remain in me, and I in them, will produce much fruit" (John 15:5 NLT).

Having an active prayer life, then, isn't about rattling off a list of wants and desires. It is, if you recall, a chance for us to partner with the One who made us, to receive encouragement, direction, joy, peace, and wisdom for our lives. It's a chance for us to produce much fruit. Fruit that makes others long for what we have. Fruit that shows the world what being a Christian is really about.

So how's your own prayer life? This week, as you've been reading about the benefits of regular conversation with God, are you encouraged to start having those conversations a little bit more regularly? Are you compelled to listen more and talk less, or to ask God's insight on things you might previously have tried to handle on your own?

William H. P. Faunce puts it this way: "No man can follow Christ and go astray."

Prayer, as you've no doubt figured out, helps us follow Christ in a new, living, and active way. As we're promised in Proverbs 8:17 (NLT): "Those who search for me will surely find me," and prayer is great place to find exactly who—and what—you're searching for.

So what kind of conversations are you having today?

There's an old joke that a woman hasn't fully committed to attending an event until she's decided what she's going to wear to it.

Laugh if you want, but there's a deeper message here: Showing up often involves a level of preplanning and dedication.

And that's true on Sunday mornings as much as it is any other time of the week. So consider this: When it comes to attending church, is your assumption that you'll be there every week, and everything else must work around that commitment? Or is your thought that you'll go as long as you don't have too much else to do? This week's readings in *Treasures of the Transformed Life* focus on presence, an important concept for any Christian.

To help explain why, let's go over this week's Scripture verse, introduced in the Sunday school/small group meeting: "since we are all one body in Christ, we belong to each other, and each of us needs all the others" (Rom. 12:5 NLT).

Notice the part that says, "each of us needs all the others." It's hoped that the next time you consider missing worship service, that phrase will stick in your mind. See, we need to be careful about the idea that we go to church just so we can get something out of it. Going to church also offers us an opportunity for us to give.

What kind of church would we be if every member—every single member—showed up on Sunday with the thought, *Who can I bless today?* or *How can I serve?*

No doubt, it would be a place where needs were met. It would be a place of joy, excitement, and selflessness. And it would be a place in which everyone felt that they fit. As journalist and author Jane Howard once said, "Call it a clan, call it a network, call it a tribe, call it a family. Whatever you call it, whoever you are, you need one."

And it, apparently, needs you, too.

Newsletter article #4.
Modifiable text available on CD-ROM toolkit.

Sooner or later, you'll discover it.

It's not some new math, some twisted form of algebra, or even a modified version of addition and subtraction; Instead, it's often described as "God math," and it defies all sorts of human logic.

It works like this: You give money to the church or to someone in need, even though you don't really have it to give. You make a sacrifice. God then does a miraculous thing: Since you've done his business, he takes care of yours. You find that your own need is satisfied, sometimes in a surprising way.

Anne Frank summed it up in this week's lesson from *Treasures of the Transformed Life*: "No one has ever become poor by giving."

Did you ever wonder why?

It could be that being generous with our finances allows us to be rich in faith. The more we see "God math" in our own lives, the more confident we become that God really will meet all of our needs.

Besides all that, though, giving a regular tithe demonstrates to God that we consider him more important than we consider money. It keeps us from allowing money to become an idol in our lives. Have you ever thought about it that way?

The truth is, God doesn't just want our cash—even if does help fund church programs and ministries. What he really wants is our hearts. He wants us to turn to him and say, "Whatever I have, it's yours."

Consider the Scripture verse presented in this week's Sunday school/small group meeting: "What can I offer the Lord for all he has done for me?" (Ps. 116:12 NLT).

It reminds us that we can never pay back God for his great gifts to us. One thing we can do, however, is cheerfully start with the tithe, the very least he asks of us. Set aside that 10 percent every week as soon as you get a paycheck, and you'll never miss it. It will show God that you're serious about putting him first—and it will continue to give him opportunities to supply your every need, just as he promised he would.

In the classic movie *White Christmas*, a rather cynical Bob Wallace (played by Bing Crosby) tells Betty Haynes (played by Rosemary Clooney), "Everybody's got an angle." Everybody, he thinks, is looking out for himself first, making sure his own needs are met, regardless of anyone else's.

That movie was made back in 1954, but some things never change, do they? We live in a selfish society, one in which each person keeps his eyes on his individual prize. And that's exactly why an excited, motivated, God-led, selfless Christian can have such a significant impact.

This week, *Treasures of the Transformed Life* addresses the topic of service, and it's so much more than just making sure that all of the items on the church's to-do list are marked off through volunteer activities. Serving others actually gives us an opportunity to be more like Jesus, the most selfless servant of all. Here's a reminder through this week's Scripture verse, introduced in this week's Sunday school/small group meeting: "I, the Son of Man, came here not to be served but to serve others, and to give my life as a ransom for many" (Matt. 20:28 NLT).

When we truly understand the depths of what God has done for us, our natural response is to do something in return. The beautiful thing, though, is that he has uniquely gifted us with different passions and interests, so we can bless him—and bless others—through things we can enjoy. Service doesn't have to be drudgery.

Someone who likes to sing, for example, might find a place of service in the church choir. Someone who enjoys kids could plug into the children's ministry. And someone who likes to organize could find a place in the food pantry or church office.

The difference between serving in the church and serving in the world, however, is the expectation of what we'll get in return. Just as Bing Crosby said, a lot of people really do have an angle, expecting recognition or reward for their time and effort.

So what about you? What are the places you serve, and what are the reasons you do so?

Newsletter article #6.
Modifiable text available on CD-ROM toolkit.

Remember being a kid and waiting expectantly during the days leading up to Christmas? You were probably on your best behavior, making sure that if Santa really did check that list twice, you'd be on the right side of it. Hours felt like days, and days felt like weeks, until the moment finally arrived: Christmas morning.

If you were like most children, you probably hopped out of bed before dawn, before your parents were even awake, and headed expectantly for the gifts wrapped and waiting under the tree. Who knew what wonders awaited?

This week, as we read through the last part of *Treasures of the Transformed Life*, we're headed toward another wonderfully special event: Commitment Sunday. That's the day you'll be able to commit your prayers, presence, service, and financial gifts to the church for the coming season. And just like Christmas morning, you have no idea what wonders await.

See, God always meets us where we are. And any time we take a step closer to him, he responds likewise by stepping closer to us. When we're ready to say yes to all that he asks of us, we can know for certain that he will richly reward us for it, and continue to draw us closer into relationship with him.

This Sunday, even if you feel the tiniest bit apprehensive about taking the next step, rely on your faith to get you there. Consider what Vincent Van Gogh said about doubt in this week's study: "If you hear a voice within you say 'You are not a painter,' then by all means paint, and that voice will be silenced."

The master painter, the one who created you with beautiful strokes of his brush, awaits. So as your special day arrives, greet it with expectancy and know that God will honor your new levels of commitment and help you stand firm. Keep this in mind:

> And now, just as you accepted Christ Jesus as your Lord, you must continue to live in obedience to him. Let your roots grow down into him and draw up nourishment from him, so you will grow in faith, strong and vigorous in the truth you were taught. Let your lives overflow with thanksgiving for all he has done.
>
> —Colossians 2:6–7 (NLT)

Fires burn brightly only as long as they're stoked.

This past Sunday, you had the opportunity to commit to new levels in your relationship with God. You boldly filled out your card, and in a wave of momentum, turned in it.

Had any second thoughts since? Had any doubts that you'll actually be able to meet that financial commitment, or fit that area of service into your busy schedule? That's not such a bad thing. It means that you've given God room to work and that without new dependence on him, it's not going to happen.

God delights in our dependence on him, you know. He waits for us to ask for help. But when we have all the answers already or we do things in our own strength, we leave no opportunity for him to be glorified. It becomes about what we can do, rather than what he can do through us.

In coming weeks, as the lessons of *Treasures of the Transformed Life* settle into your consciousness, it will be possible for you to lose steam and to forget what it was all about. On the other hand, you could take what you've learned and build on it.

Remember that very first chapter, the one that talked about not even realizing your thirst? Over the past forty days, you gained new insight into how thirsty you really were, and discovered that the only thing that will really satisfy is pure, living water, poured into your life through consistent prayer, Bible study, acts of service, fellowship with other Christians, and regular financial gifts.

That kind of water is not the type that puts out a fire. Rather, it's the kind that stokes it, and allows us to burn so brightly that we draw others to us like moths to a flame. So what will you do to keep that fire burning brightly, keeping the principles of the last few weeks in the forefront?

How about this? The next time you see a glass of water—and every time thereafter—you'll be compelled to take a long, satisfying drink. It is that living water that transforms us, until that day when we don't even recognize who we used to be.

Newsletter article #8.
Modifiable text available on CD-ROM toolkit.

transformed living

Church Name
Church Address
Church Phone

Yes, I am/we are ready to dive in—connecting more with others, acting as God's hands and feet on earth, and serving enthusiastically. Therefore, I/we commit to serve in the following areas in the coming year.

	M	F
Administrative (Office help, finances, library, mailings, answer phone, etc.)	( )	( )
Adult Ministry (Sunday school, small groups, classes, men's or women's ministry activities, etc.)	( )	( )
Church Building and Grounds Care (Gardening, maintenance, housekeeping, painting, etc.)	( )	( )
Communications (Web site, newsletter, photo or videography, publicity, sign messages, etc.)	( )	( )
Congregational Care (Visit homebound, hospitals; meals; assist seniors, etc.)	( )	( )
Evangelism (Follow up with visitors, new member assimilation, organize attendance records)	( )	( )
Fellowship Activities (Book club, work with senior adults, churchwide retreat, etc.)	( )	( )
Hospitality (Usher, greeter, follow up with visitors, parking, etc.)	( )	( )
Music/Arts (Choir, drama, play handbell choir, assist children's music, etc.)	( )	( )
Nursery (Childcare, Mother's Day Out, etc.)	( )	( )
Outreach (Food pantry, clothing ministry, Volunteers in Mission, children's center, etc.)	( )	( )
Prayer Ministry (Prayer tree, prayer vigils, coordinate prayer requests, etc.)	( )	( )
Student Ministry (Teach or assist grades K–5, middle school, Vacation Bible School, etc.)	( )	( )
Wednesday Night Activities (Kitchen, clean up, serve food, lead class, etc.)	( )	( )
Worship (Prepare communion, lay reader, altar preparation, flowers, etc.)	( )	( )
Youth (Assist with meetings, chaperone trips, events, etc.)	( )	( )
Wherever the church needs me	( )	( )
Other_____	( )	( )

Transformed Living Service Commitment

Name: _____ Name: _____

E-mail Address: _____ E-mail Address: _____

Cell Number: _____ Cell Number: _____

Home Address: _____

Home Phone Number: _____

Signed _____ Signed _____

transformed
living

Transformed Living
Service Commitment

[Year]

Church Name
Church Address
Church Phone

Yes, I am/we are ready to dive in! I/we want to connect more with others, act as God's hands and feet on earth, and serve enthusiastically. Therefore, I/we commit to serve in the following areas in the coming year.

Welcoming (Evangelism)
M   F
1 ( ) ( ) Parking lot greeter
          (_____ service time)
2 ( ) ( ) Greeter (_____ service time)
3 ( ) ( ) Usher (_____ service time)
4 ( ) ( ) Follow up with visitors
5 ( ) ( ) Adopt a new member
6 ( ) ( ) Assemble new member packets
7 ( ) ( ) Other_____

Learning
8 ( ) ( ) Attend _____ class
9 ( ) ( ) Participate in *Walk to Emmaus*
10 ( ) ( ) Attend Sunday school
11 ( ) ( ) Attend Wednesday Bible study
12 ( ) ( ) Attend *DISCIPLE Bible Study*
13 ( ) ( ) Attend new members' class
14 ( ) ( ) Other_____

Discipleship
15 ( ) ( ) Invite a friend to church
16 ( ) ( ) Learn to share my faith
17 ( ) ( ) Lead a small group study
18 ( ) ( ) Lead where needed, if qualified
19 ( ) ( ) Other_____

Administrative
20 ( ) ( ) Help in office
21 ( ) ( ) Maintain bulletin boards
22 ( ) ( ) Assist in library
23 ( ) ( ) Work on history committee
24 ( ) ( ) Other_____

Nursery Ministry
25 ( ) ( ) Early service nursery helper
           (Sunday school)
26 ( ) ( ) Later service nursery helper
           (Worship)
27 ( ) ( ) Wednesday service volunteer
28 ( ) ( ) Mother's Day Out
29 ( ) ( ) Other_____

Student Ministry
30 ( ) ( ) Teach K–1st grade
31 ( ) ( ) Teach 2nd – 3rd grade
32 ( ) ( ) Teach 4th –5th grade
33 ( ) ( ) Assist in elementary grades
34 ( ) ( ) Teach middle school

M   F
35 ( ) ( ) Teach high school
36 ( ) ( ) Assist in middle/high
           school classes
37 ( ) ( ) Teach/help with vacation
           Bible school
38 ( ) ( ) Assist with activities for K–5
39 ( ) ( ) I have a special skill or interest I'd
           like to share with children:
           _____
40 ( ) ( ) Other_____

Youth
41 ( ) ( ) Volunteer for Sunday youth
           meeting
42 ( ) ( ) Volunteer for youth program
43 ( ) ( ) Chaperone mission trip
44 ( ) ( ) Chaperone youth trip
45 ( ) ( ) Work with youth on ongoing basis
46 ( ) ( ) Other_____

Adult Ministry
47 ( ) ( ) Teach an adult class
48 ( ) ( ) Establish/lead new adult class
49 ( ) ( ) Participate in small group
50 ( ) ( ) Lead small group
51 ( ) ( ) Participate in women's ministries
52 ( ) ( ) Participate in men's ministries
53 ( ) ( ) Other_____

Wednesday Night Activities
54 ( ) ( ) Kitchen committee
55 ( ) ( ) Assist with children's
           programming
56 ( ) ( ) Youth helper
57 ( ) ( ) Lead adult class
58 ( ) ( ) Help serve food
59 ( ) ( ) Help clean up
60 ( ) ( ) Collect money
61 ( ) ( ) Close and lock building
62 ( ) ( ) Other_____

Worship
63 ( ) ( ) Lay reader
64 ( ) ( ) Altar arrangement coordination
65 ( ) ( ) Prepare sanctuary for Sundays
66 ( ) ( ) Restock pew supplies
67 ( ) ( ) Communion preparation

Service commitment form—long version, page 1.
Modifiable text in MS Word available on CD-ROM toolkit.

transformed living

Church Name
Church Address
Church Phone

Yes, I am ready to dive in—connecting more with others, acting as God's hands and feet on earth, and serving enthusiastically. Therefore, I commit to serve in the following areas in the coming year.

Youth Choir (Attend rehearsals, sing as scheduled, choir tours as scheduled) ( )
Contemporary Worship Committee (Help plan contemporary worship events) ( )
Song Leader (Lead hymns in contemporary worship) ( )
Youth Communications (Web site, newsletter, photo or videography, publicity, sign messages, etc.) ( )
Sound System Volunteer (Operate sound systems at Sunday morning worship or at youth worship events) ( )
Instrumental Musician (Play a musical instrument in worship or at special events) ( )
Acolyte (Light candles or help lead Sunday worship or other worship events) ( )
Youth Evangelism (Follow up with visitors, make newcomers feel welcome) ( )
Liturgical Dancers (Perform at worship services or special services; *practice scheduled as necessary*) ( )
Youth Hospitality (Help with refreshments on Sunday morning or at youth events) ( )
Music/Arts (Choir, drama, handbell choir, assist children's music, etc.) ( )
Church Nursery (Help in church nursery on Sundays or other times; *requires special training*) ( )
Outreach Activities (Half-day or full-day local mission projects for youth) ( )
Prayer Ministry (Prayer tree, prayer vigils, coordinate prayer requests, etc.) ( )
Tutoring Ministry (Assist another student in a subject area in which you are strong) ( )
Youth Mentor (Mentor younger youth by being a friend, inviting them to events, etc.) ( )
Church Usher (Usher at the church's main Sunday morning services) ( )
Lay Reader (Read Scripture at church's main Sunday morning services or youth worship services) ( )
Church Maintenance (Assist in church maintenance projects, yard work, landscaping, etc.) ( )
Wherever the church needs me ( )
Other_____ ( )

Youth Service Commitment

Name: _____

E-mail Address: _____

Cell Phone Number: _____

Home Address: _____

Home Phone Number: _____

Signed: _____

transformed living

i'm/we're ready to dive in!

please print:

name(s) _____

address _____

city, state, zip _____

signature(s) _____

❏ my/our commitment to prayer is to pray for our church and other needs _____ times each week

❏ my/our commitment to presence this year is to attend worship service _____ times each month

❏ my/our commitment to gifts is to give to this church $ _____ per *circle one* (week / month / year)

❏ my/our commitment to service is to volunteer this year in the area(s) checked on the separate service commitment form

---

transformed living

i'm ready to dive in!

YOUTH COMMITMENT CARD

please print:

name _____

address _____

city, state, zip _____

signature _____

❏ my commitment to prayer is to pray for our church _____ times each week

❏ my commitment to presence this year is to attend worship service _____ times each month and youth activities _____ times each month

❏ my commitment to gifts is to give to this church $ _____ per *circle one* (week / month / year)

❏ my commitment to service is to volunteer this year in the area(s) checked on the service commitment form.

---

transformed living

I'm ready to dive in!

Children's Commitment Card

please print:

name _____

address _____

city, state, zip _____

signature _____

❏ I will pray for my family, friends, church, and world.

❏ I will attend worship and Sunday school.

❏ I will give to this church.

$ _____ per circle one (week / month / year)

❏ I will serve this year!

❏ I will sing in my age group choir.

❏ I will bring my Bible to church.

❏ I will attend children's activities.

Commitment cards.
Adobe PDF graphic files available on CD-ROM toolkit.